To

St. Joseph's Monastery

Library -

from

C. T. Kobbé -

1936 -

MOTHER MARIANNE OF MOLOKAI

THE MACMILLAN COMPANY
NEW YORK · BOSTON · CHICAGO · DALLAS
ATLANTA · SAN FRANCISCO

MACMILLAN & CO., Limited
LONDON · BOMBAY · CALCUTTA
MELBOURNE

THE MACMILLAN COMPANY
OF CANADA, Limited
TORONTO

MOTHER MARIANNE OF MOLOKAI

MOTHER MARIANNE
OF MOLOKAI

BY

L. V. JACKS

NEW YORK
THE MACMILLAN COMPANY
1935

B
M

SET UP BY BROWN BROTHERS LINOTYPERS
PRINTED IN THE UNITED STATES OF AMERICA
BY THE FERRIS PRINTING COMPANY

TO

THE SISTERS OF SAINT FRANCIS
who have given their lives to the service of lepers
in the Hawaiian Islands

REVEREND SISTER MARIANNE
Matron of the Bishop Home, Kalaupapa

To see the infinite pity of this place,
The mangled limb, the devastated face,
The innocent sufferers smiling at the rod,
A fool were tempted to deny his God.

He sees, and shrinks; but if he look again,
Lo, beauty springing from the breast of pain!—
He marks the sisters on the painful shores,
And even a fool is silent and adores.

(Signed) ROBERT LOUIS STEVENSON.

Kalawao, May 22nd, 1889.

Reverend Sister Maryanne
　　Matron of the Bishop Home
　　　　Kalapapa.

To see the infinite pity of this place,
The mangled limb, the devastated face,
The innocent sufferers smiling at the rod,
A fool were tempted to deny his god.

He sees, and shrinks; But if he look again,
Lo, beauty springing from the breast of pain! —
He marks the sisters on the painful shores,
And even a fool is silent and adores

　　　　　　　　Robert Louis Stevenson

Kalawao May 22ᵈ 1889

PREFACE

THERE are several commonly employed systems of biographical writing. One is the so-called psychological manner, in which the biographer endeavors amongst other things to explain by various methods the mental processes of the person discussed. Another theory lays stress upon the dramatic, and in consequence collects and arranges material with a view to producing effect appropriate to the stage.

But here the method is simply to relate facts as they occurred, with such comment as circumstances may demand for a full understanding. Unless discussion seemed necessary, the writer has avoided dissertations upon individual happenings.

In the matter of chronological order no attempt has been made to deviate from ordinary time sequence. There are no throwbacks as the fiction writers call them, and no effort to anticipate events. Relation is kept as nearly as possible in a closely synchronized order that tallies with actual occurrence.

The material from which this book is compiled is of varied quality, but it is in immense quantity.

Preface

There is no attempt to give a full bibliography (an exhaustive bibliography upon the study of leprosy would fill a large volume by itself), but among the Appendices is a small select bibliography, with some accompanying notations. The book is founded roughly on three kinds of documents. First, the personal correspondence of Mother Marianne Kopp. These letters were taken from the archives of the Franciscan Sisters of Syracuse, New York, and kindly furnished to the writer. Second, the journal of Sister Leopoldina Burns, the only Sister now living who was among the early arrivals in Franciscan missionary work in the Hawaiian Islands, and who was in the very first group of volunteers to go to Molokai. The journal that Sister Leopoldina wrote begins in 1887 and makes a loosely knitted but continuous narrative till 1918.

There remains a third group of documents composed of many published accounts of social, political, religious, and medical activities in Hawaii, and of the study and treatment of leprosy and kindred matters, which I have used where need arose.

The amount of dependable published material about Mother Marianne is scanty. A few articles have appeared in periodicals, but it seems that most of this writing is copy work, in which one reporter after another has borrowed from newspaper stories, repeating well-known facts, but adding little new or of lasting value.

Accompanying Mother Marianne's letters are the letters of various officials to her, and some other correspondence and papers that were of importance to the Sisters in getting established in the islands.

Chief reliance however rests upon Mother Marianne's own letters and the journal of Sister Leopoldina. There are no published accounts that reveal the story so clearly as these documents.

FOREWORD

THIS book was undertaken at the suggestion of Dr. Roy J. Deferrari, Dean of the Graduate School, Catholic University of America, and owes much to his advice. He placed freely at my disposal notes and materials resulting from his research which have greatly lessened many difficulties. To him is owing a debt of gratitude not merely in the present occasion but in others extending to the years in which I was a graduate student with him, so that the usual formal acknowledgment does not adequately convey the obligation.

The Sisters of Saint Francis of Syracuse, New York, have generously opened their archives, and given me some of their most valued records; books, papers, reports, both personal and official correspondence, photographs, and charters, a total of 309 documents, many never before published, many never before shown to anyone. Without this kindness the story would be at best superficial and incomplete. It still has numerous shortcomings, for which however no one except the writer is responsible. But if the career and accomplishments of the brilliant and deserving woman who is the subject of this study are, even in an imperfect manner, brought closer to the attention of that intelligent public which admires courage and sagacity and reverences charity as a great virtue, the effort expended is well repaid.

L. V. JACKS.

Creighton University,
Omaha, Nebraska,
April, 1934.

CONTENTS

Contents

MOTHER MARIANNE OF MOLOKAI

I

EARLY LIFE

PICTURE the little province of Hesse Darmstadt toward the beginning of the last century. The tide of Napoleonic armies has receded but a generation ago. Peace has come to the little grassy valleys and long rugged hills, and the inhabitants settling gradually into the elder ways of living after the twenty-three years of war that followed the French revolution, are content to live close to their soil and to wrest from it their livelihood. The Rhine, an ancient blue highway slipping silently along, winds around crag and headland, across valley and plain, as it did in Drusus' day. And indeed just beyond the border of Hesse at Bingen local pride refers to a Drusus Tower, a Drusus Bridge, and a Drusus Well. Certainly the Romans built a fort there about A.D. 70, and military roads to Cologne and Trier.

Many centuries have gone down the stream since the bronze armored and helmeted legionaries with their scarlet and black crests first marched over these hills on their way to the Oder and the misty northern ocean. The strong little men from the south, stocky, and dark, and quick-eyed, were destined to leave a permanent print of their visit upon that strange palimpsest which is the Rhine valley. And, still dimly to be seen and deciphered beneath the writings of succeeding ages, is their firm original mark, a scrawl that spells arched bridges and paved roads, strong stone houses and temples, corn, olive and grape, grammar and history and the beginnings of science. In his cheerful provincial way, Ausonius their poet celebrates the beauties of the Rhine and the Moselle, the goodness of Rhine wine, the kindness of Rhineland people.

Gaul, Roman, German, Hun, Goth, Vandal, Frank, and Saxon have in turn waged war on these picturesque pine-fringed hills, and battles and expeditions, cities and empires have come and gone, while something of the earnestness and endeavor of these weary generations seems bred into the Hessian people, for they are serious and sober, thrifty and industrious. In the midst of this background rich in history, richer in legend, a child could begin life in innumerable fine deeply laid influences of cultural and social significance.

But when January sweeps across the Rhine and the wind howls, and the great curtains of snow ride high and white in air like Odin's daughters searching for warriors' souls, and the evergreens are but dim spear-pointed, storm-tossed shapes, covered with frost, the hardy Hessians have need of their hot blood and sturdy courage.

On the twenty-third day of January, 1836, in the little town of Heppenheim of Hesse Darmstadt, was born a baby destined to a career as interesting and as unusual as any in the romantic centuries that preceded. She was christened Barbara. Her father was Peter Kopp and her mother Barbara Witzenbacher Kopp. The baby could not have retained a conscious memory of the pleasant Hessian land with its shadowy forests and little high-roofed villages, its winding streamlets and terraced vineyards and intensely cultivated fields, for when Barbara was about a year and a half old, the spirit of adventure prompted an emigration, and her family moved to America and settled in Utica, New York. Yet she always felt very kindly toward the country of her birth, a predisposition due to family recollections often related to the youngsters, and to that usually strong family solidarity that affects so many better-class immigrants.

It was always her wish, as one learns again and again from those associated with her, that no publicity of any kind should accrue to her or her work. She accordingly said little about herself and her tasks, and her friends through fear of giving offence to one so dearly loved, remained reticent during her life. Only after her death, did they speak freely, at a time when no earthly benefit could fall to her lot, and when possibly much good could be accomplished on earth by a presentation of her example.

But even then they relate little about her early life, if indeed they know much about it. Her existence, after she became a religious, developed so much worth-while accomplishment and such great interest to the human heart that bleeds for afflicted brethren, that little attention has been given to the time before she departed for Hawaii. For the sake of completeness, and in the hope that it may help to a better understanding of her work as a missionary, the main facts of her early history, in so far as one is able to gather them, follow here.

Her resolve to enter upon a religious life seems to have appeared in childhood. How it developed, and how it found furtherance, are not clear. It became simply a question of when she could properly relinquish the responsibilities of her home to take up her life's work. Her mother died, leaving the father, two brothers, Matthew and John, and four girls, Elizabeth, Catherine, Eva, and Barbara, later Mother Marianne. Although still a young girl she undertook to manage the home as if it were a right upon which she entered. These responsibilities at so early an age did much to mature her mind. They probably also induced that sobriety of view, and that extremely practical skill in dealing with persons that later distinguished her.

But if children are the product of their people, the people themselves are a product of innumerable varying circumstances, of many generations of breeding, and of vast effect springing from environment. And something of the many vicissitudes her homeland had experienced must have been deep ingrained within her soul, for her fortitude, her judgment, her patience, and her foresight, extraordinary in her maturity, were already visible in her childhood.

At last she felt free to go her own way. The Kopp family was sufficiently grown to be independent, and the children had to some extent scattered from the paternal roof; according to the recollections of distant relatives both parents were dead when Barbara entered the convent. The necessity of abandoning the home which she had kept together must have seemed a trying ordeal, but she made her way to St. Anthony's Convent, of the Sisters of the Third Order of St. Francis, in Syracuse, N. Y., and on November 19, 1862, at the age of twenty-six, she was invested by the Very Reverend Father Leopold, Commissary General of the Order of St. Francis, in St. Mary's Church, Syracuse, N. Y. She underwent her novitiate training in St. Francis' Convent, Syracuse, N. Y., under the direction of the Reverend Mother M. Antonia Eulenstein, and was professed with the name Marianne on November 19, 1863, in the Church of the Assumption in Syracuse, N. Y. Her work as a religious begins in the school of this parish.

This woman's ability as an administrator showed itself clearly to her superiors from the outset. In the various accounts of her labors in the foreign missions, as reported by co-workers, one is impressed by her calmness and good sense, her firmness and kind heart, and her eminent ability to obtain the coöperation and good will not only of the religious members of her group, but of all others with whom her daily work brought her in contact. The most obstreperous leper, from both awe and loving respect, wilted before her quiet but strong personality. Government officials rarely, and only with genuine reluctance, denied requests she made, because these requests came always from the highest good judgment, and always in the interests of the poor wretches for whom she worked. Accordingly, her religious life, almost from the moment that she made her profession, is a series of administrative appointments, culminating in her charge of the missions in Hawaii.[1]

On August 2, 1875, she became superior of St. Joseph's Hospital, Syracuse, and this election had

[1] Cf. Appendix A.

[6]

approval from the Very Reverend Father Provincial. Here, in addition to the experience of administering an important and large activity of her Order, she gained much practical information which later she put to good use in Hawaii. In fact, her interest in the well-being of St. Joseph's Hospital remained with her always. Although greatly concerned about all whom she left behind, she never failed in letters from Hawaii to show special interest in the progress and personnel of St. Joseph's Hospital. Thus, in a letter to Mother Bernardine from Kalaupapa, Molokai, on May 6, 1889, a very interesting letter which tells among other matters of the death of Father Damien, we read: "I trust you are enjoying good health and that the Hospital is in prosperous condition. Sister Bonaventure and the Sisters who have lately come speak so much of your beautiful hospital that it makes me long to see it. Have you many patients, and who are your doctors? Remember me kindly to those of my acquaintance."

On December 27, 1877, Mother Marianne became Provincial Superior at the Provincial Chapter. At the Provincial Chapter of July 14, 1881, she won reëlection as Provincial Superior by a unanimous vote, and this office she was holding when the call came for volunteer workers in the leper missions of Hawaii.

II

HAWAII AND THE CATHOLIC MISSIONS

It is not the present purpose to enter upon a detailed description of Hawaii and the Catholic missions. Some general notions, however, of the work in these islands, especially among the lepers of the region, are necessary, in order that one may properly appreciate the contribution of the Franciscan Sisters of Syracuse and of Mother Marianne in particular.

The Hawaiian Islands, formerly called Sandwich Islands, are situated in the Pacific Ocean between 18° 55′ and 22° 2′ north latitude, and 150° 47′ and 160° 14′ 40″ west longitude. There are eight greater and several smaller with a northwest to southeast trend, and they are partly coral and partly of volcanic origin. Only seven of these islands, however, are generally inhabited, and these are, in the geographical order from west to east, Niihau, Kauai, Oahu, on which Honolulu the capital city is situated, Molokai, Lanai, Maui, and Hawaii.

The earliest known visit to these islands from the outside world occurred in 1778-79 when the British explorer Captain Cook touched at Kauai and Hawaii with his vessels the *Discovery* and the *Resolution*. He found them inhabited by the Polynesian race, which ethnologists have since called the Sawaiori, because its principal representatives are the *Sa*-moans, the Ha-*waii*ans, and the Ma-*ori* of New Zealand. But impenetrable mystery shrouds the origin of the Polynesian race. At the present time the population of these islands is very heterogeneous. Native Hawaiians still maintain predominance, but both Japanese and Chinese nearly equal them. Portuguese too are numerous, Americans and British representing other important national groups. Through intermarriage of all races with the natives, the number of part-Hawaiians has grown large, and it is practically impossible to estimate it with any dependable degree of accuracy.

Representatives of the clergy of "The Congregation of the Sacred Hearts of Jesus and Mary and of the Perpetual Adoration of the Most Blessed Sacrament" often called the Picpus Fathers, because they were founded in a home on Picpus Street, Paris, had arrived as early as July, 1827, and by the time of the arrival of the Franciscan sisters had spread their labors throughout the islands.

Constructive work for the benefit of the unfortunate lepers was very much in its infancy. In order to stop the spread of the loathsome disease the Hawaiian government had established a settlement for the lepers on the island of Molokai. During the first year of the enforcement of segregation the condition of the poor lepers was physically as well as morally a truly wretched one. They received their rations from the government, more or less regularly, and that was all. But some knowledge of the disease of leprosy is proper at this point that one may appreciate the efforts of those who labored amongst its victims.

Since Magellan spread his canvas to the Pacific breeze, northern minds have been busy with the South Seas, their strange inhabitants, and the good and bad things to be found there. With the passage of time the last geographical barriers of land and ocean have yielded to the persistent exploration of bold spirits, and now the mind of man is driven to seek for other and subtler fields. Cancer and radium, electricity and sound, insanity and light; such variegated objects call to the research worker today, and the man who ventures into their regions is venturing upon just as bold a quest as was Sir John Mandeville.

Some of these barriers to the realm of science yield readily, and the only obstacles opposed to man are the vastness of the subject and the ironic brevity of human life. But other problems resist with baffling

tenacity, and though surrounded by cunning attackers, hold out firmly and are made to yield only
by slowest degrees and in scantiest measure. Scattered widely in the green islets of the South Seas but
heavily concentrated in Hawaii lies an enemy more
insidious than cancer, and no whit less horrible in
its ravages.

There is an innate terror for many people in the
very name of leprosy. It is certainly one of the most
ancient of diseases. It was a deadly foe in the Orient
when the Jews were but a tiny and unknown tribe,
when the Achaian soldiers assembled at Aulis for the
siege of Troy. It was considered a scourge from the
very gods; the Jews saw in it a visible sign of Jeho-
vah's displeasure and the positive sinfulness of the
possessor; and up and down Asia, as far as men
roamed, the leper bore the name "unclean." Men
thrust him forth from association with his fellows,
condemned him to die an outcast, denied him all consolation and assistance.

Even the rawest tyro cannot fail to see there is
something peculiarly dreadful in the approach of this
mysterious disease. For mysterious indeed is the correct term to apply to it. It is of all known diseases
one of the slowest to make itself manifest. But, pro-
portionately, it is one of the most difficult to eradi-
cate, if, in truth, it is ever eradicated. Moreover, it

works in inscrutable and incalculable ways. Father Damien lived amongst lepers, contracted the disease, and died. The nuns who also worked and lived amongst lepers for some forty-seven years have never had a case. There is a record of a clean native on Molokai who married successively two leprous women and had children by both. He lived and died untainted by leprosy, and all the children were clean, but each mother died of the disease. It is a strange affliction. It seems at certain periods to rage, then again, unaccountably, to lapse. In some patients it causes fearful agony. Others sink into a lethargic condition, and see their members decay and fall from the body without experiencing very much suffering.

The uncertainties in the progress of the destroyer are only equalled by its fearful rate of fatality when it does seize a victim. Lepers find no cure. They die. Hence the dreadful panic amongst the survivors, hence often their shivering unwillingness to go amongst the unclean ones. (Among the Hawaiians, however, are many honorable exceptions to this rule.) Hence, the imperative need for aid and assistance from the outside.

The traveler on the upper Magdalena or on some remote branch of the Amazon may walk along a quiet jungle path, and see on all sides tall trunks of trees and swinging thick vines, huge creepers, graceful lianas; and his untrained eye, dizzied by the profusion of colors, grays, browns, and whites on the bark, innumerable greens in the foliage, streaks of gold where the sun comes through, wanders leisurely over the scene, until an uneasy sixth sense tells him all is not well. He hesitates before going farther, stands fast, and looks and looks; then suddenly one of the great swaying lianas is galvanized into strange life. It hangs down but it squirms, lights dart along its smooth surface. The startled watcher is now aware of a head and great jewel-like eyes, and before his astounded gaze the constrictor fairly leaps into life. Its vast muscles ripple and it draws itself back up to the bough from which it had been swinging down waiting for a victim to pass underneath. Few enemies are more dreaded by the natives than the great silent serpents, the very incarnation of quiet, of preternatural stealth, of watchfulness, of merciless destruction. The parallel is well founded as the Hawaiians have learned to their sorrow, for their valleys and glens hold a lurking enemy as deadly as the constrictor and a thousand times harder to defend against.

The onslaught of leprosy was a terrible thing to the native, though to do him justice, he has borne his burden with a stoical courage above praising. The brown man was not without means to combat his normal enemies, numerous though they were. But this was a new and strange scourge that invaded his islands, as it were on the wings of the dawn, and presently spread right and left among the helpless Hawaiians. The brown man had courage and sagacity. He could fish and hunt. He could swim like an eel. He cared little for storms. He could stay under water for minutes, and on it for many, many hours. In his frail canoe he performed voyages of almost unbelievable length across the turbulent ocean from one cluster of atolls to another. He caught fish, he slept on the warm sand in the sun, he subsisted on bread fruit, taro, and poi. He caught crabs and shellfish and devoured them. He was hardy, patient, stoical, and shrewd. He could read the stars and the sun, he knew the signs of wind and storm and sea and heaven.

But before leprosy he stood like one crushed.

Not, indeed, that it frightened him. It does not frighten the native, to this day. But segregation was the only resource his mind could conceive, a remedy indeed as good as the best cultivated intellect could devise; a remedy fair enough after its fashion, but making life a slow and awful tragedy to the victim thus set aside.

When even among the best medical men divisions of opinion appear, as regards this extraordinary visitation and the means of combating it, the native and the layman may be pardoned if their approach to the subject seems halting and at times incomplete.

The medical profession has still a great deal to learn about leprosy. It has done much to alleviate the physical suffering of the unfortunate victims, but it cannot claim as yet to have discovered a cure. Some cases that seem to have attained a cure present grave doubts as to the identity of the original ailment. The general method of combating the plague is still to isolate the victim, and, while exerting every effort to make him comfortable, to permit the disease to spend itself on him. This method has succeeded in practically eliminating the curse from Europe, and bids fair to eliminate it from other parts of the world as well.[1]

Leprosy may have had its origin in India, on the evidence of a passage in the Rig Veda (circa 1400 B.C.) which describes a disease that could be leprosy. Others ascribe its beginning to Egypt, on the basis of a description of a disease similar to leprosy found in the "Ebers papyrus" (circa 1300 B.C.). It has frequent mention in the Bible, *e.g.,* Exodus, 4.6; Numbers, 12.10; 4 Kings 5; although the description in Leviticus, 13.13 is regarded by many physicians to-day as not applicable to true leprosy. From the fact

[1] Cf. Appendix B.

that men traditionally called it the "Phœnician disease" it would seem that Asia is its real home.

It is well established that leprosy came to Europe from Egypt in the first century B.C. with the legions of Pompey. Many centuries later, it spread yet more widely over Europe in the wake of returning crusaders, so that in the fourteenth century twenty thousand asylums cared for the lepers. In France alone there were nearly two thousand such leprosaries, and it is said that at one period nearly one-third of the population of England had leprosy. As a result of the most drastic measures of isolation the disease began to decrease in the fourteenth century and by the fifteenth century had practically disappeared from Europe as a whole. It is thought that the Chinese introduced leprosy into the Hawaiian Islands nearly one hundred years ago. Many have attributed it to the Portuguese whalers who used to make Hawaiian ports to replenish supplies and for recreation. The Gulf coast region is the only place in the United States in which it shows a tendency to spread, but government health reports show it has commenced sporadically in many other areas. The disease prevails through South and Central America with the possible exception of Chile. It also appears in Australia, New Caledonia, and the islands of the far South Pacific.

An acid-fast bacillus which rather closely resembles the tubercle bacillus, morphologically, as well as tinctorially, causes leprosy. Dr. Hansen of Christiania, Norway, first discovered this bacillus in 1871, and fully reported it in 1874. Much of our knowledge of its characteristics is due to Neisser. The leprosy bacilli occur in profusion in the granulomatous tissue of the corium and subcutaneous structures of the leprous nodules, chiefly within cells called "lepra cells"; and within endothelial and connective-tissue cells, as well as lying free, packed in lymphatic channels, the so-called "globi."

There is a consensus of opinion that every case of leprosy owes its origin to contact, direct or indirect, with some other case, but evidence as to the exact manner in which this takes place is to a great extent lacking. It is an error, however, because of this lack of evidence to say, as some have said, that leprosy is not contagious. As regards those living for a long time in attendance upon lepers, there exist comparatively few instances of the contraction of leprosy as in the case of Father Damien at Molokai. This of course may follow from any of several reasons, such as the conditions under which they labored, these conditions being notoriously wretched in the case of Father Damien, or the personal precautions which individuals assumed against contracting the disease.

In the case of the little band of workers with Mother Marianne, it was known that the one reward for her labors which she asked was that none of her Sisters should contract the disease; and no one of them thus far has ever suffered it. The strongest proof that leprosy is to some extent contagious, is the fact that a partial victory over it, in various parts of the world, notably Europe, has come only by segregating those afflicted and permitting the plague to run out its course in the restricted area. If one takes a child from its leprous parents and surroundings immediately after birth, there is little or no likelihood of its developing leprosy, but a delay of a few months is often fatal.

It will not benefit the narrative to enlarge upon the many and varied theories regarding the origin and transmission of this dreadful scourge. Nor does the specific treatment of the ailment in modern times concern us here. Since the discovery of the leprosy bacillus all efforts of medical research workers have gone to discover some specific prescription which will counteract this bacillus, and in this labor attention still dwells upon chaulmoogra oil, and in subcutaneous injections this has given promise of being most permanently helpful.

The books at the hospital in Molokai show that the leper settlement opened January 6, 1856, although writers commonly make it a year earlier. The settlement commenced with a hundred and forty-one lepers of whom a hundred and three were males and thirty-eight females. The mortality for the year was twenty-six. On September 4, 1873, the year when Father Damien arrived, eight hundred and nine inmates were on the records. While conditions in the settlement at this time were vastly improved, they were still far from being decent. Father Damien gives the following description of the settlement, at the time of his arrival, and some of the improvements made, in an official report which he addressed to the president of the board of health, in March, 1886, just two years before the arrival of Mother Marianne and her two assistants, Sister Leopoldina and Sister Crescentia.

"By a special providence of our Lord, Who, during His life showed a particular sympathy for the lepers, my way was traced to Kalawao in May, A.D. 1873. I was then thirty-three years of age, enjoying a robust good health,— Lunalillo being at that time king of the Hawaiian Islands, and His Excellency E. O. Hall, president of the Board of Health.

"A great many lepers had arrived lately from the different islands; they numbered eight hundred and sixteen. Some of them were old acquaintances of mine from Hawaii, where I was previously stationed as a missionary priest; to the majority I was a stranger.

Mother Marianne of Molokai

"The Kalaupapa landing was at that time a somewhat deserted village of three or four wooden cottages and a few old grass houses. The lepers were allowed to go there only on the days when a vessel arrived; they were all living at Kalawao—about eighty of them in the hospital—in the same buildings we see there today. All the other lepers with a very few kokuas (helpers) had taken their abode further up toward the valley. They had cut down the old Pandanus or penhala groves to build their houses, though a great many had nothing but branches of castor oil trees with which to construct their small shelters. These frail frames were covered with ki leaves (Dracaena terminalis), or with sugar cane leaves,—the best ones with pili grass. I myself was sheltered during several weeks under the single pandanus tree which is preserved up to the present in the church yard. Under such primitive roofs were living pell mell, without distinction of age or sex, old or new cases, all more or less strangers to one another, these unfortunate outcasts of society. They passed their time with playing cards, hula (native dances), drinking fermented ki root beer, home-made alcohol, and with the sequel of all this. Their clothes were far from being clean and decent on account of the scarcity of water, which had to be brought at that time from a great distance.

"The smell of their filth, mixed with exhalation of their sores, was simply disgusting and unbearable to a newcomer. Many a time in fulfilling my priestly duties at their domiciles, I have been compelled not only to close my nostrils, but to run outside to breathe the fresh air. To protect my legs from a peculiar itching which I usually experienced every evening after my visiting them, I had to beg a friend

of mine to send me a pair of heavy boots. As an antidote
to counteract the bad smell, I made myself accustomed to
the use of tobacco, whereupon the smell of the pipe preserved me somewhat from carrying in my clothes the
obnoxious odor of the lepers. At that time the progress of
the disease was fearful, and the rate of mortality very
high. . . .

"In previous years, having nothing but small damp huts,
nearly all of the lepers were prostrated on their beds, covered with scabs and ugly sores, and had the appearance of
very weak broken down constitutions. In the year 1874
the great question was—how to improve the habitations
of the unfortunate people, the government appropriations
being at that time barely enough to provide them with
food.

"During that winter a heavy south wind blew down the
majority of their half-rotten abodes, and many a weak
leper lay there in the wind and rain, with his blanket and
clothes damp and wet. In a few days the old grass beneath
their sleeping mats began to emit a very unpleasant vapor.
I at once called the attention of our sympathizing agent to
the fact, and very soon there arrived several schooner loads
of scantling to build solid frames with. All lepers who
were in distress received on application the necessary material for the erection of frames, with one inch square laths
to thatch the grass or sugar cane leaves to. Afterward rough
boards arrived, and also the old material of the former
Kaliki hospital. From private and charitable sources we
received shingles and flooring. Those who had a little
money hired their own carpenters; for those without means,
the priest with his leper boys, did the work of erecting a

good many small houses. Besides, some newcomers who had means built their dwellings at their own expense."

Further on in the same report, Father Damien discusses the morality of the settlement.

"I feel myself obliged to beg leave of your Excellency to be allowed to speak of a very serious matter, in which I officially appear as one of the principal agents. To avoid criticism I will with a liberal mind lay aside as much as possible all differences of opinion, and show how needful a step has been taken for the temporal and eternal welfare of our lepers by drawing a parallel between the past and the present, and between those who yield and do not yield to moral training.

"Previous to my arrival here, it was acknowledged and spoken of in the public papers as well as in private letters, that the greatest want of the lepers at Kalawao then was not having a spiritual leader or priest, the consequence of which was that vice as a general rule existed instead of virtue, and degradation of the lowest type went ahead as a leader in the community. On the arrival of a new number of lepers, the old ones were soon at work to impress them with the erroneous axiom 'Aole kanawai ma keia wahi'—(in this place there is no law). Not only in private conversation but in public meetings, I myself heard this doctrine proclaimed; and for a long time, indeed, I was obliged to fight against its application being made to the divine law as well as to the human law. In consequence of this impious theory, the people, mostly unmarried, or separated on account of this disease, were living promiscuously, without distinction of sex, and many an unfortunate woman had to become a prostitute to obtain friends who would take care of her, and the children, when well and strong, were used as servants. When once the disease prostrated them, such women and children were cast out, and had to find some other shelter; sometimes they were laid behind a stone wall, and left there to die, and at other times a hired hand would carry them to the hospital. The so-much praised 'Aloha' of the natives was entirely lacking here, at least in this respect.

"As already mentioned in other pages, the Hawaiian hula was organized after the pagan fashion, under the protection of the old pagan deity Laka who had his numerous altars and sacrifices, and I candidly confess I had hard work to annihilate Laka's religion, and worship, and thereby to put a stop to the hula and its bad consequences. Though the people had reached a climax of despair, both of soul and body, may it be said to their honor, that I had found them less addicted to sorcery and the doings of the 'kahuna lapaau' or native doctors than I had found the old natives of Hawaii—circumstances which encouraged me much to stay permanently among them, with the quasi-certain hope of my ultimate success as a Catholic priest.

"By a short digression, I will here speak of another source of immorality, viz., the evil effect of intoxication. I first have to explain how they have obtained the material. There grows very abundantly along the foot of the mountains a plant which the natives call ki (Dracaena terminalis), the root of which, when cooked, fermented, and distilled, gives a highly intoxicating liquid. The process of distilling being very crude and imperfect, produces, naturally enough, a liquid which is totally unfit for drinking.

[23]

A short time after my arrival, the distilling of this horrid liquid was carried on to a great extent. Those natives who fell under the influence of it would forget all decency, and run about in a nude condition, acting as if they were totally mad. The consequences can be easier imagined than written on paper. The local authorities have endeavored to stop all these horrible proceedings, but for a long time they were unsuccessful. It being discovered that certain members of our police were in league with the evil doers, the 'buna-nui' and myself went round, and both by threats and persuasion, they finally delivered up their implements which were used for distilling. Some of the most guilty perpetrators were convicted, but were pardoned under the condition never to do it again.

"For a long time, as above stated, under the influence of this pernicious liquor, they would neglect everything else, except the hula, prostitution, and drinking. As they had no spiritual adviser, they would hasten along the road to complete ruin. A good many of the sick and prostrate were left lying there to take care of themselves, and several of them died for want of assistance, whilst those who should have given a helping hand were going around seeking enjoyment of the most pernicious and immoral kind.

"As there were so many dying people, my priestly duty toward them often gave me the opportunity to visit them at their domiciles, and though my exhortations were specially addressed to the prostrated, often they would fall on the ears of public sinners, who, little by little, became conscious of the consequences of their wicked lives, and began to reform, and thus with the hope in a merciful Saviour, gave up their loose habits.

"Kindness to all, charity to the needy, a sympathizing hand to the sufferers and the dying, in conjunction with a solid religious instruction to my listeners, have been my constant means to introduce moral habits among the lepers. One of the great moral improvements which helped to do away with licentiousness was the granting of intermarriage licenses between lepers who were not prevented from marriage by a previous marriage tie, and many a couple are today living at the settlement in a decent manner.

"I am happy to say, that, assisted by the local administration, my labors here, which seemed almost in vain, at the beginning, have thanks to a kind Providence been greatly crowned with success, as, at present, there are very little if any at all, of the above-mentioned evils committed."

Father Damien was too sanguine, as Mother Marianne's experiences proved, but he had sowed the good seed, and in very truth it was germinating rapidly and well. He had long prayed that Sisters might come to assist in his work on Molokai, particularly among the leprous women and children. He felt that with Sisters permanently established in the settlement the continuance of the work after his death would remain assured. This prayer was soon answered.

III

THE SUMMONS TO HAWAII

Walter M. Gibson, Minister of Foreign Affairs and president of the Board of Health in the little kingdom of Hawaii, a tremendous power with King Kalakaua and Queen Kapiolani, once said "If a noble Christian priest, preacher, or sister should be inspired to go and sacrifice a life to console these poor wretches (the lepers) that would be a royal soul to shine forever on a throne reared by human love." This was in the beginning of 1873.

Later in this year, May 13, 1873, Mr. Gibson wrote in the editorial column of the native paper, *Nuhou*, on hearing of Father Damien's decision to devote the remainder of his life to the lepers, "We have often said that the poor outcast lepers of Molokai, without pastor or physician, afforded an opportunity for the exercise of a noble Christian heroism, and we are happy to say that the hero has been found. When the *Kilauea* touched at Kalawao last Saturday, Monseigneur Maigret and Father Damien, a Belgian

priest, went ashore. The venerable Bishop addressed
the lepers with many comforting words, and introduced to them the good father, who had volunteered
to live with them and for them. Father Damien
formed this resolution at the time, and was left
ashore among the lepers without a home or a change
of clothing except such as the lepers offer. We care
not what this man's theology may be, he is surely a
Christian hero."

Mr. Gibson and Father Damien also soon realized, to use Mr. Gibson's own words at the dedica-
tion of the Kapiolani Home for girls of leprous
parents, that the lepers "were afflicted with a disease
so peculiarly objectionable in its character and conditions that to cope with it, with any possibilities of relief, it was not alone sufficient to be provided with
skilled physicians and remedies, but with experienced
and devoted nurses—especially women, endowed
with that rare devotion to the cause of the sick and
the suffering that arises solely from the highest inspiration of Christian charity. The hope was enter-
tained that possibly some of those self-sacrificing
religious women, who devoted their lives to the care
of the lepers in such institutions as that of Tracadie in
Canada, might be induced to exercise their great
charity in these islands."

Mr. Gibson, with the approval of the King and

Queen, accordingly addressed a letter to His Excellency Bishop Herman Koeckemann, Bishop of Olba, dated January 4, 1883, in which he very politely, in the name of Christian charity, asked him to bring to the Hawaiian Islands members of some one of the Catholic sisterhoods to nurse the lepers. Mr. Gibson subsequently referred to this letter in a public address, and even quoted from it as follows: "My Lord, as I am aware that eminent institutions of charity, such as I have referred to, and which this country needs, abound in the Catholic church; and as I feel assured that your representation would be all influential, I make an appeal, and offer an invitation through you, to sisters of charity of your church, to come to the help of the sick of this country; and I doubt not I may proffer to them in advance the profound obligation and gracious recognition of Their Majesties, the thanks of His Majesty's government, and the blessings of the Hawaiian people. . . ."

The Bishop responded promptly and favorably, and designated the Reverend P. Leonor as the agent to go forth on a mission to seek the much-needed help; and His Majesty, the King of Hawaii, gave him a royal commission to assist him in his quest. Father Leonor landed in San Francisco, and traveling eastward, made application to more than fifty different religious sisterhoods before he reached St.

Anthony's Convent of the Sisters of the Third Order of St. Francis in Syracuse, N. Y.

Mother Marianne was then Provincial Superior, and as soon as she had met the visiting priest, and learned the nature and purpose of his quest, she expressed herself as quite prepared to accept the work, provided the members of her community would acquiesce. She accordingly summoned the Sisters and novices in a solemn Chapter of the sisterhood, and Father Leonor addressed them. Sister Leopoldina, then a novice, relates how Father Leonor in desperation, with trembling voice and tearful eyes, described the great need of Sisters among the lepers, and his long discouraging attempt to find these Sisters. His first ray of hope had come from Mother Marianne.

The Sisters and novices retired, and the usual summons for volunteers followed. Twenty-four of the Sisters and nearly all of the novices expressed their willingness to devote themselves to this work, and wrote their names on the list. The needs at home were so great, however, that they could spare only six Sisters besides Mother Marianne. It was never the intention of the community that Mother Marianne should go as a permanent member of the group. Since she insisted that as Superior of the convent it was her duty to go with the first group of

Sisters, and see them well established in their new project, for she was also Provincial Superior of the community at that time, the members were willing that she should go, but only on condition that she return as soon as the Sisters were well and definitely settled.

Thus, as an eye witness tells us, on a bright clear morning of October (October 23, 1883) at about seven o'clock, Mother Marianne Kopp, and six Sisters, Sister M. Bonaventure Caraher, Sister M. Crescentia Eilers, Sister M. Renata Nash, Sister M. Rosalia McLaughlin, Sister M. Ludovica Gibbons, and Sister M. Antonella Murphy, together with a Miss Molloy, a cousin of Sister Bonaventure, set out on the long journey to Hawaii. To Mother Marianne, then past forty-five, it could not have appealed as would adventure to more youthful minds, and the falling red and gold leaves of autumn and the tang of frost betokening the waning year, were a subtle omen that she too was setting out upon a sere and autumnal journey from which she would not return. The members of the community, and numerous friends, gathered about the departing ones, some of the Sisters still endeavoring to persuade Mother Marianne that she should not go. They felt with perhaps truer premonitions than they realized, that once she found herself in the midst of such a tremendous labor as this promised to be, she would never come back to them. The parting was sad. Sister Crescentia later said she could never forget Mother Bernardine, standing there as the train moved away, with arms outstretched and face pale and drawn, while the Sisters gathered around to comfort her.

It is impossible to appreciate in any way adequately what this parting meant unless one recalls the then existing knowledge of leprosy. Leprosy meant an incurable mangling and rotting away of the body, horrible beyond words. It was believed to be easily and readily transmitted, and to give up one's life to the care of the lepers was tantamount to entering upon a slow process of death, a death of indescribable suffering.

The decision was taken. The engine puffed, the train pulled out, and the volunteers were gone. They had hardly left the station when Mother Marianne discovered she had mislaid her pocketbook. She left the train at the next station, returned, and was in the midst of the startled friends while they still grieved for her. She laughed at their amazement, encouraged them by her cheerfulness, and took the next train west, to overtake her party on the following day.

In San Francisco a priest met the group and conducted Mother Marianne and three of her companions to Mercy Hospital, the other three to the convent of the Sisters of the Presentation. While waiting for their boat to leave, the Sisters enjoyed several days of quiet rest. On a Thursday afternoon they boarded the little steamship *Mariposa* for the last part of their long journey. The sea at first was calm and delightful, but later the *Mariposa* was tossing and pitching, and all were sick. On the third day out all except Mother Marianne were well again, and enjoying the sea air, but she was sick during the entire voyage. In fact, while in Hawaii being under necessity at times, in the interest of her missions, to make trips on the rough and treacherous sea about the Hawaiian Islands, she suffered much from this affliction.

On the Wednesday following their departure, when still some distance from Honolulu, a pilot boat flying the royal colors approached, and all began to wonder what royalty on board the *Mariposa* was about to receive a royal escort. Presently a priest became visible on the boat. He was Father Leonor. He shouted, "Are the Sisters on board?" On receiving the answer "Yes," the pilot boat veered around, and was soon out of sight hastening back to Honolulu to announce the good news to King Kalakaua and Queen Kapiolani.

Honolulu is the only very good harbor in all the

islands. As one approaches it, a sharp pointed ridge of rock with its barren sides shuts out the view of the city of Honolulu. This is Diamond Head, an extinct volcano, from whose crest it is still possible to look down into an immense crater, now only a cavern, but once freighted with death. Within the city itself, Diamond Head is ever present, either on one side or the other, as one travels about. As the *Mariposa* entered the harbor, and touched at the landing, November 8, 1883, the bells of the city began to ring, and crowds of people gathered at the wharf to greet the Sisters who were to relieve the spiritual and physical suffering of their dear ones. Four royal carriages, polished and shining, with liveried drivers, were present to receive them.

Queen Kapiolani's first lady in state, since the Queen herself was indisposed at the time, was present to greet the Sisters officially. Their escort led them through the streets, Mother Marianne with the Queen's first lady in the first carriage, and the other Sisters in those following. The bells continued to ring joyfully, and shouts of welcome reached them from all sides.

At last they drew up in front of the cathedral, where Bishop Herman Koeckemann, many priests and brothers, and the acolytes, were waiting to welcome them. After receiving the Bishop's blessing,

Mother Marianne and the Sisters went through a crowded church to the front of the altar, where reserved seats awaited them. The Bishop addressed them impressively and explained to the people the nature of the work which the Sisters of St. Francis had come to Hawaii to do. He emphasized that the Sisters need expect neither praise nor gratitude, but many crosses and much suffering. Not from any failing in the Hawaiian character, but rather because of the general weaknesses of the human race, those last words of Bishop Herman proved most true. The many records and notes of the Sisters are replete with examples of ingratitude, but with it are also numerous examples of Christian repentance and noble lives and deaths. It is evident throughout the activities of Mother Marianne and her companions that the one great recompense for all their trials and sufferings, the one great stimulus to carry on against almost overwhelming odds, was the number of conversions and the edifying attitudes at death which they were instrumental in bringing about. Benediction of the Blessed Sacrament followed Bishop Herman's talk, after which the Sisters of the Sacred Hearts of Jesus and Mary received the newcomers.

IV

THE BRANCH HOSPITAL

THE excitement and strain of the trip were over, and business of serious nature waited. Queen Kapiolani proved an interesting if naïve friend. When she shook hands with Mother Marianne she left a one hundred dollar bill in the Sister's hand, somewhat to Mother Marianne's astonishment. This was on an occasion some days later, when Mother Marianne and another Sister went to the royal residence for a request visit.

The two women must have held a deep interest for each other. Queen Kapiolani had curly dark hair, dark eyes, and a high forehead, with the bluff sturdy features of her race. Physically she was large and massive, with that deplorable tendency so many Polynesian women show to become excessively heavy. She had a rather fleshy nose, a long strong jaw, and a thick neck. She was undoubtedly capable of very serious thought, which tended at times to merge into brooding melancholy, and indeed the fortunes of her people, both politically and hygienically, were not of a sort to make her cheerful.

She saw across from her a woman of an altogether different type, a woman heir to all the culture of many generations of German efficiency and understanding. Mother Marianne had gray eyes and the straight-direct gaze of the thinker who concentrates upon the heart of a problem, and brushes aside all such details as are essentially unimportant. Not quite so large a woman as the Queen and much slenderer, she had that balanced power and energy proceeding from strong intellectual control, and that intrepid courage and quiet accompanying a union of emotional conviction and sound logic. The European mind, shrewd, thoughtful, and resourceful, expressed itself in the finely modeled lines of Mother Marianne's mouth, a feature wherein the will or lack of it so often depicts itself, the straight strong nose and clear eyes; above all in the perfect repose of manner.

The two had much to say to each other, and parted in mutual admiration.

Mother Marianne took up work at once at what was then known as the Branch Hospital at Kakaako, Honolulu. She began here on January 11, 1884. This original Branch Hospital had a rather curious origin. A mile or more out of Honolulu was a large salt marsh that at high tide was flooded, and at low tide a sticky mire. This space was diked off and drained, and in this territory the hospital was built, surrounded by a very high, tight, strong wooden fence, somewhat after the fashion of the old palisaded fences that defended our western forts in the late 1700's, and closed by heavy and well-padlocked gates.

Within the enclosure stood several buildings, one of them, long and narrow, extended seaward, beyond solid diked ground, so that its outer end stood on pilings, and at high tide the sea rushed beneath the floors, surging and coiling about the supports.

A Mr. Van Gieson was in charge when Mother Marianne came. Conditions seem to have been very bad. Sister Leopoldina does not say this in her accounts, but from descriptions she gives, there is reason to suspect that some of the funds provided for the lepers were diverted to the pockets of people who cared for the victims.

Food was served to Sisters by the lepers, and sanitary conditions generally were appalling. Appeals to Van Gieson for better arrangements brought no satisfactory results. But the men who delivered milk to the hospital managed, on their own initiative, to make some minor alterations in the program of handling goods, and this helped the case a little.

There were then over two hundred patients in the Branch Hospital, a place exclusively for lepers; men and women crowded together in a fashion that modern authorities would not permit in the worst prison. Since most of us nowadays are prone to think about hospitals in terms of massive buildings, sterilized and gleaming apparatus, brilliant lighting, splendid operating rooms, a score of eminent surgeons and physicians, another score of internes and orderlies, and still other scores of starched nurses at call, and all in an atmosphere of cleanliness, respectability and germicide that fairly staggers the layman, it is well to pause here for a moment, and to revise our theories of hospitals while thinking of this Branch Hospital. It was a cluster of rickety wooden buildings, some connected, some unconnected, with no central heating plant, no lighting except God's good sun and a few oil lamps, no toilet and drainage facilities such as exist now fifty years after; exposed to all the winds of heaven and the Pacific, stuck in the middle of a barren yard, and surrounded by a fence which gave it a strong savor of the penitentiary appearance. The great stock of drugs and implements which we consider essential to the equipment of the modern hospital was conspicuous by its absence. The kitchen was presided over by ulcerous lepers, and the heating, such as it was, and that was scanty, was attended to by other lepers, who fired up the small stoves when they had fuel. It is noteworthy that even in this mild climate there were days when the inmates were blue with the cold; though comparatively little fire would have relieved them.

This was the objective that greeted the Sisters.

Van Gieson had had two cells built for solitary confinement punishment. The cells were so small (not more than four by four) that no one could lie down; and if one should forcibly thrust two or three men into such a spot, nobody could sit down. The Kanaka's natural dread of darkness and solitude, added to the disease, was enough to make prisoners go mad.

Men put in for disorderly conduct sometimes remained five or six days at a stretch, a refinement of cruelty that resembles some monstrous tale out of the Arabian Nights; it is a touch quite Mongolian, a story that might have come from the court of Genghiz or the camp of Hologu.

Van Gieson's right-hand man was Tom Burch, a large half-native, father Irish, mother Hawaiian. He made a good policeman, though of violent and unreasoning temper. There is something grimly reminiscent of Kipling's story "Namgay Doola" in the adventures of Tom Burch. The rule of Van Gieson and Burch was not, generally, well received amongst the lepers, but that made little difference, for the outside world as a rule did not care so much just what the lepers thought.

The Sisters applied themselves to elementary work, chiefly scrubbing and sterilizing, and gradually got the place cleaned up. In January, 1884, Mother Marianne received information from Mr. Gibson that the Queen wanted her to open a new hospital in Wailuku on the island of Maui. The Board of Health added its request. On January 22, 1884, Mother Marianne went, taking Sisters Renata and Antonella.

They had a rough voyage over to Maui. The vessel, like most little fore-and-aft coasting schooners, ran under bare poles half the time, for she could hardly carry a rag of sail, so violent was the storm. They reached Maaleea Bay late that evening, in such a hurricane that they could not dock. Kanaka sailors lifted their passengers into a small boat nevertheless, and pushed off, but could not row to shore. The boat tossed. The Sisters were drenched in the rain, the spray, and the waves that broke over them; it was pitch dark, and only after supreme efforts did these skillful natives at last get to the pier at midnight. Footing under the pilings was nowhere to be found, and the boatmen seized the Sisters and hoisted them bodily to the planks above. As the pier was long and narrow, extending far out into the sea, and completely swept by tremendous rollers, it was hardly safer than the boat they had just quitted, and they clung to it desperately to escape being borne back into the sea.

At last they got off the dock to solid ground, and found a carriage to take them to Wailuku. Seven miles in intense darkness, over stones, roots, fallen branches, and holes. The horses proceeded at a pace not much better than a walk, and the Sisters between the combined effects of cold, exposure, soaking in salt sea brine, and hunger and weariness, were nearly dead. This was an ordeal that would have taxed experienced combat soldiers, used to all the exigencies of modern warfare in wintry seasons; for the women thus exposed it was almost death. Sisters Renata and Antonella were seriously sick after this trip, and indeed Sister Antonella seemed never entirely well thereafter. Mother Marianne rallied quickly, and showed no outward signs of injury. An indomitable spirit supplied the needed strength.

They arrived at the Malulani Hospital in the early hours of the morning. The next day, with the irresponsible vigor of the tropics, the weather changed, and was extraordinarily beautiful; a cloudless sky, a sun of surpassing splendor, a fair breeze, and far in the background of their scene the bulk of

Haleakala, perhaps the largest extinct volcano in the world; by summer a vast green cone ten thousand feet in height, in winter capped with snow while the lowlands still sweltered in heat.

Mother Marianne, on the occasion of Queen Kapiolani's visit some two months later, asked her to name the new building. Kapiolani gave it the Hawaiian name Malulani, signifying "under the protection of heaven." The Sisters took formal charge on April 24, 1884. All sick who had no contagious diseases found care in this hospital. The Sisters also opened a grade school mostly for native children.

But work here again was of elementary fashion, and shortly after the christening of the hospital, Bishop Herman wrote to Mother Marianne to return to Honolulu. This was something of a shock to her, and she dreaded to leave the two sick Sisters. It was with serious misgivings that she set out.

During Mother Marianne's absence, affairs at the Branch Hospital in Kakaako, Honolulu, had grown steadily worse. The lepers were certainly disorderly, and it does not appear that Van Gieson and Burch kept very good discipline, but as is usually the case in such tangled affairs where there is much mutual criticism and recrimination, there was something to be said on each side.

Sister Crescentia had been left generally in charge during the absence of Mother Marianne, but her authority was hard to extend or to enforce. Affairs reached a difficult point when Van Gieson asked Sister Crescentia to approve a severe punishment for a leprous woman detected, as he said, in adultery. Sister Crescentia bluntly asked where the man might be, and got no satisfaction, Van Gieson remarking that the man must have run away. Whereupon, suggesting that it was a case of two or none, Sister Crescentia refused to approve the punishment. Van Gieson nevertheless had the native put in "solitary" but apparently made no effort to apprehend her companion.

As might be expected there was an extremely unsatisfactory moral and sanitary tone in the crowded leper stockade, gambling, thieving, and opium smoking ran close competition for frequency with the adultery that so disturbed Van Gieson.

A climax occurred one dark still night when nine of the more able-bodied leprous men crept into his cottage and attacked Van Gieson with clubs. He shrieked, intervention by the Sisters caused confusion among the attackers, and he got clear of his swarming enemies, and fled. It was, apparently, this uproar that caused Bishop Herman to bring Mother Marianne back from the island of Maui. After such a commotion, the Sisters naturally and rightly complained to both the Bishop and Mr. Gibson.

The nine lepers were of course arrested, and five put in one of the four by four cells, and four men in the other. Sister Crescentia took them blankets and tried to win their confidence. Mr. Gibson thought they should be deported to Molokai. This exile struck the lepers very much as Siberian banishment once did certain Russian classes; they regarded it as a sentence of imminent death.

When Mother Marianne returned to Honolulu, she appointed Sister Bonaventure to take charge of the Malulani Hospital, and the good Sister departed at once on her mission. She held the post, incidentally, for more than twenty years, and gained universal esteem.

The lepers in the Branch Hospital now alleged so many charges against Van Gieson that Mr. Gibson finally removed him from his Honolulu office, giving him a position on Molokai. Mother Marianne, freed from his embarrassing and noisy interference, presently won the natives to a complete docility; proving that kindness, persuasion, and genuine good will frequently work wonders.

Many new factors however augmented her problems. It does not appear, in spite of the government's undoubtedly earnest desire to help, that it

The Branch Hospital

A curious case evolved during the first months the Sisters were in the Branch Hospital. They had a very neglected little negro girl called Ellen Davis, about ten years old, who had been put amongst the lepers, apparently as though thoroughly contaminated. They kept her under observation, like the others, but she showed no symptoms. Following the persistent scrubbings and ministrations of Sister Crescentia, she presently emerged from her previous shell of grime, into the outer air, and learned a rigid cleanliness. Nevertheless, once the suspicion of leprosy had tainted her, even though her original ailment was probably only some minor skin disease, it was exceedingly hard to get out of the stockade, and Ellen spent no less than five years in the Branch Hospital before the Sisters finally secured her discharge as a non-leper.

In a letter dated August 31, 1884, to her superiors at home, Mother Marianne writes:

"You have every reason to think that I am wilfully neglecting you, but I beg to assure you that such is not the case, and that only want of time is the cause of my silence with you. I would gladly send you a letter by every steamer leaving this Port, if time would favor me to write as often. You know, dear Mother, what it is to have charge of an Hospital.

"We have almost constantly two hundred sick here

afflicted with a horrible disease; in a strange country among strange people, and are responsible to a government for our transactions. From this you may judge that we have our hands full, and our heads too. Sometimes our duties are very trying, but God is good to us, and helps us out of all difficulties. I think it is all owing to the good prayers of our dear ones at home."

Further in the same letter one reads:

"Accept my heartfelt thanks for your kind namesday letter, and for the pretty little book containing such delicious thoughts for a hungry tired soul. Mine is both. . . ."

In an effort to raise the general morale of the inmates, which never climbed high and sank often to rock bottom, Mother Marianne planned to make Christmas in Honolulu something of an event. The Sisters made simple brown cotton dresses trimmed with turkey red for all the girl inmates, and with the dining room scrubbed to real cleanliness, Mr. Gibson provided a Christmas dinner that rivaled the old native feasts.

But trouble with Tom Burch flared up again and reached a climax shortly after the holidays. Native policemen had little liking for him, but Mother Marianne, reasoning like a true diplomat that it was better to maintain the *status quo* and to work out details peaceably in quiet negotiations, managed to suppress their critical remarks till one night when an attractive little Chino-Hawaiian girl called Julia, about sixteen years old, came missing at roll call. One of the Hawaiian policemen indicating Burch's door with his night stick, said to Mother Marianne "He has her in there."

The Superior felt a certain indignation. She went straight to the door, and turned the knob. The door was locked. She said in a gentle voice, "Open the door, please." There was not a sound.

Mother Marianne had that deeply essential quality in every great leader, she could be hard as steel at a pinch. When she spoke again to say "Tom Burch, open this door at once," her order rang with that tone known to every field marshal from Arminius to Moltke, and Burch bounding up, whirled the key, and flung open the door, to emerge like a maddened leopard.

In the light of the native policeman's lantern, his face was black with anger, the veins and cords in his great throat rigid, eyes glaring, and he stood towering over Mother Marianne as if ready to strike her down. He was a big man, and like many big men with small souls, liked to stand close when dealing with anyone shorter, so as to force the smaller person to look up to him.

"Tom Burch," she said, "you can be policeman no longer. Give me the keys."

Burch went into a frenzy, jumping, stamping, and cursing, but he was a coward at heart. He took refuge in a gesture of desperation, and with a tremendous sweep of his powerful arm hurled the keys through the window, and far out into the ocean. Then his ebullient passions suddenly evaporated, he turned away, and stalked out.

Mother Marianne took the leper girl by the hand, and they walked back in silence to the sick girls' ward. Some of the best of the Hawaiian divers, and their best are very good indeed, combed the sea next morning for the lost keys, but only failure waited upon their efforts.

Because of the panic fears that leprosy everywhere evoked, it was excessively difficult to get anyone to do housework, or for that matter, any kind of assistant labor, where the disease-ridden lepers were involved. As the year wore on, Mother Marianne became extremely anxious to procure some assistance, more particularly in doing the heavier labor about the hospital, for much of it was beyond the strength of the already overtasked women concerned.

There remained also to be considered the matter of her return to Syracuse, for she had quitted her community with the understanding prevalent that when she had definitely established the Hawaiian leper missions she would return to New York. But the need for her in Hawaii grew greater day by day, and on February 12, 1885, Bishop Herman Koeckemann, in a letter to the Very Reverend Father Joseph M. Lesen, struck the root of the situation. "I hear that you are occupied with the question, whether the Rev. Moth. Marianne shall remain here or return home. You will pardon the liberty I take to tell you most decidedly, that we consider the presence of Mother Marianne quite necessary for the success of your colony in these Islands. Besides her many excellent qualifications, certainly fully known to you, she has learned by personal experience how to deal with persons and circumstances in her rather complicated position, and she enjoys the highest esteem and full confidence of all she has to deal with."

It became clear that more Sisters would have to come out from Syracuse. And the prospect of Mother Marianne's return to New York grew slenderer as months elapsed. Once more the opportunity for sacrifice offered itself. Sisters Benedicta, Martha, Charles, and Leopoldina were the second group to come.

By this time it had begun to be well apparent to Mother Marianne's shrewd observation that leprosy is to some extent, in the layman's phraseology, a disease of dirt and carelessness, and that strict attention to cleanliness, regular and correct dressing, and the proper use of antiseptics, with a careful avoidance of unnecessary contacts, will enormously diminish the chances of infection.

The confidence she had felt increased and rose higher, and indeed circumstances bore out her logic, for none of her Sisters ever contracted the disease, and they worked and lived continuously amongst hideous cases; nor have any of their successors had the disease to this day.

The second contingent arrived in San Francisco on Sunday morning, April 12, 1885, sailed on the *Alameda* April 15, and reached Honolulu on April 22. They had had an uneventful voyage to Hawaii, and as soon as possible after landing, went on duty at the Branch Hospital.

Of the several physicians who attended the lepers and conducted experiments in the study of the disease, Doctor Arning ranked among the best liked. He had been to Molokai, and gave Mother Marianne some gruesome accounts of the new babies in the hands of leper parents, stories which practically decided that good woman to attempt their rescue and aid. Doctor Arning was likewise the first to bring her the sad news that Father Damien whom so far she knew only as the resident priest of the lepers on Molokai had himself become a leper.

Visitors at the Branch Hospital were not frequent; the fear of contagion explaining this phenomenon readily enough.

It would be alike foreign to the nature of Mother Marianne's life and services, and to the purpose of this narrative, were her days represented as exciting and tense, even though the continued presence of imminent death does produce always a certain tension. Life, rather, passed in great cycles, bounded by the slow swing of the brilliant tropic planets, and the rise and fall of long seasons; it was a very deliberate symphony, slowly played out against the background of soft sound provided by the Pacific, a never-ending rumble which, like cannon fire to second-line soldiers, reminds them that an inflexible barrier intervenes between them and home. Life was far from monotonous, but it was strictly circumscribed, within cruelly narrow limits.

Queen Kapiolani visited the hospital at intervals, apparently actuated by an unusual sense of duty, but these royal visits provided little of great importance to the lepers whose cases were already in many instances beyond relief. The royal visit resulted, at all events, in a pardon for some of the gamblers who had previously been sentenced to Molokai. Part-Hawaiians in particular, whose nervous systems responded with startling speed to the slightest stimuli, proved extremely bad subjects for games of chance. The management of the Branch Hospital, dreading anything that might increase these susceptibilities, and particularly anxious to avoid those periods of profound psychological depression that so often overtook the moody sufferers, made persistent efforts to break up gambling games. But they found themselves continually balked by the stealth and furtiveness of their patients.

Conditions on Molokai continued to be the burden of many gloomy stories that filtered back to Kakaako and the Branch Hospital. Men sent there regarded their journey not only as a consequence of leprosy but as a punishment. The island was still looked upon with that shuddering horror which in English prisons once accompanied mention of Van Diemen's Land, and more modernly in French reformatories, the Devil's Island. Not all the lepers sent to Molokai were merely lepers; the opium addict, the poor pickpocket, the habitual drunkard, and the murderer, were also found in the ranks.

Because a number of the families transported to Molokai had taken their children with them, while yet other babies had been subsequently born, the matter of what to do with these youngsters was becoming an ever more pressing problem to the government. Left to the ill-regulated care of leprous parents, the likelihood that they would in turn contract the disease seemed overwhelmingly great. Equally discouraging, no education or training or scantiest moral suggestion seemed available. There were no schools in the Leper Settlement, and Father Damien, the one prop against which the whole leper colony seemed to relax to secure support, was now himself affected, and his death a question only of time. It is pathetic to note that at about this period he ceased to open his sermons with the customary word "Brethren," and instead addressed his parishioners with these words, "We lepers."

Mother Marianne called Mr. Gibson into conference, and suggested that a home for children of leper parents be built near the Sisters' residence in Honolulu. Raising money, and getting a home built, were in his opinion matters of no great difficulty, but he was at his wits' end to find help for the Sisters, both in their present hospital work and in the new tasks that loomed up over the projected home. But with conditions becoming somewhat better in the hospital, as Mother Marianne and her coadjutors kept doggedly at their tasks, the lepers had gradually come to feel less alarm and despondency, and the civil authorities thus encouraged vigorously hunted out every suspected case and brought the victim to the hospital. Consequently the place was well burdened, and the Sisters continually overworked. But Mother Marianne pushed her suggestions about the home, and it was agreed that at least the officials would try to bring all the girl children of leper parents to the Branch Hospital, where they could be put in a special building.

A square two-story house, painted gray and white, was erected near the Sisters' residence. It was formally opened on November 9, 1885. Mother Marianne christened it the Kapiolani Home, and this compliment to royal interest apparently bore good fruit. This institution lay within the inclosure at Kakaako, and hence escape from it was almost as unlikely as the escape of a leper from the hospital proper. A twelve-foot veranda, essential in that climate, extended around three sides of the building, which contained a schoolroom, storeroom, kitchen, and dining room on the first floor, and two large dormitories and a room for a matron on the upper floor. Every effort was made to insure cleanliness, from the well-painted walls to the iron beds.

On the opening day Queen Kapiolani presented the keys of the Home to Mother Marianne, saying: "I deliver these keys to you." And when she had accepted them, King David Kalakaua stepped forward and, inviting her to a seat beside him, decorated her with the Order of Kapiolani, an order established by His Majesty chiefly to reward acts of benevolence in behalf of his people. Mother Marianne, taken by surprise, thanked His Majesty through Mr. Gibson.

The prime minister then, in a lengthy address, reviewed the circumstances leading up to the founding of the Kapiolani Home, and discussed the need. "A home was wanted especially for girls of the native race, who, being suspected of this disease, are not permitted to attend any schools, and suffer from the stigma in society. It was felt that your children who had contracted the disease, or who were barely suspected of being so afflicted, might have their lives brightened by special care and treatment, especially at the hands of the devoted Sisters of St. Francis, who came from America, inspired by their faith and love of good, to give their lives for the hope of ameliorating your condition, and especially that of your children.

"With that end in view it was deemed essential and proper to establish a 'Home' which would provide a decent shelter for your female children, especially where they could be educated and kindly treated, and where they would live comfortably contented lives, which would be otherwise denied them, if they were cast adrift with all the odium of this disease attached to them."

But when Mr. Gibson advertised for a matron, his seductive requests fell upon uninterested ears. Children from Molokai, like the guests from Gibbet Island in the old story, held no fascination whatever to white woman or Hawaiian. So finally Sister Martha detached herself from her manifold duties, and took charge of the Home.

Bringing the children from Molokai proved no light matter. Though the children themselves as yet were "clean," and the parents were ready enough to admit that continuous associations at home would very likely infect the youngsters, they still resented bitterly the efforts of the Board of Health to remedy matters. And one leprous father, by way of expressing his dissatisfaction, seized an iron dagger and drove it through the back of a policeman who had come to take his children. The victim died almost at once. The same boat that brought the children to Honolulu to the Branch Hospital and thence to the new Home, also brought the father for his trial. Naturally he was found guilty, and his sentence was simply to be returned to Molokai for life!

Ten children ranging in age from five to thirteen came in the first group. The murderer had two called Mare and Mari, strange, fierce little creatures, with stolid features, piercing black eyes, and bushy mops of hair. The youngest in this queerly assorted party, a baby, Annie, was five. One called Maka proved the most energetic and headstrong.

As might be expected, these children had not the remotest conception of order, authority, law, or discipline. They frankly informed their new friends that in the past they had always done quite as they pleased, for if dissatisfied with their own parents or with conditions at home, they could and would always run away to the mountains, where they led a life but little removed from that of young wild cats.

Anyone cynically inclined might derive a certain amusement from the efforts made to civilize and, so to speak, to rehabilitate, this group. Mr. Gibson even endeavored to produce musical instincts in them and, when the first alarm over them had worn away, persuaded a music teacher to take their training in hand.

For a while all went well enough, then one day seven of the girls were missing. The police conducted a search of Honolulu, and scouting parties took to the mountains. All to no avail. Many speculations developed as to how they got unaided over the stockade fence. Three days of this, and everyone gave up the runaways for lost. Then Annie, the five-year-old, finally felt her courage evaporate, and came to Sister Martha and said: "I know where they are."

They had crawled unobserved through a slender

hole in the foundation of the Home, and had spent the past three days lying at length, for their location on the bare ground and under the house did not permit them to sit even half-upright, in a labyrinth of dirt and cobwebs. They were gray from hunger and exhaustion when drawn out, but as far as one could observe, their indomitable spirit remained unruly as ever. The Home, however, served its purpose, the children at least received bathing and disinfections with regularity and care, though attendants had to force some of them into a bath, and ultimately they even showed traces of becoming civilized. The best and most popular of the girls in the Kapiolani Home, who was one of the original shipment from Molokai, was a pure-bred Hawaiian called Mary Joseph. She stayed with the Sisters till she was twenty-four, when she left the Home to marry a part-Hawaiian called Sullivan. All this was by way of rather light preliminary to Mother Marianne's real tasks.

In a letter dated August 28, 1886, to her superior at home, she writes:

"We have now a doctor from Japan, who makes the treatment of leprosy a specialty. He comes to the Hospital daily, and treats seventy patients; all are doing wonderfully well. He gives hot medicated baths twice daily and medicine before and after meals. The doctor's treatment increases our work but we do it cheerfully when we see such a good effect. Several patients are so much improved that the doctor thinks of discharging them soon. Which is something quite unheard of in the history of leprosy."

Not a little of the deep depression that overhung the unhappy lepers was due to the false hopes repeatedly worked up by near-cures of this sort, which after arousing wild hopes, beliefs, and speculations amongst the patients, and even some credence in the more philosophical, finally left the deluded victims precisely where they had been before—still lepers.

Then came Father Damien to Honolulu, on one of his rare visits, and at Mr. Gibson's request, the Sisters furnished him a bed in the Branch Hospital. His disease was then well advanced, his nose swollen, his ears greatly enlarged and drooping, and his face and neck purplish-red. Mother Marianne had several conversations with him during his brief stay at the Hospital, and the plan to send Sisters to Molokai was born and definitely developed. Whose idea it was at first is hard to say. Mother Marianne had been thinking along these lines for some time, and it is well known that Father Damien had wanted the Sisters to come, since some years before. When two strong minds meet on a problem in which both think in the same way, conclusions shape themselves rapidly.

The plan met immediate and loud opposition, many charitable reasons being assigned, but Mother Marianne's insistence brought the good results she so desired. As for Father Damien, he was already failing in power and energy as his leprosy took toll, and with all his intrepid spirit he wished for some such improvements as the arrival and help of the Sisters before his death.

Mother Marianne had now become definitely convinced that her final life work lay in these islands; more than that, in Molokai.

On February 16, 1887, she wrote to Father Joseph Lesen, then at Syracuse, N. Y., who had been acting as Provincial Minister to the order, and whose continuance in this position had been for some time a matter of uncertainty.

"I cannot tell you how anxiously I have waited to hear the result of your chapter, every day seemed a week till the news came; and when the news came, after a long waiting, that you, Dear Father, were again chosen to guide and direct the little Ship of the Order, we all uttered a fervent Thanks be to God, in which even good Mr. Gibson joined us; he, poor man, was, if possible, even more troubled and anxious than we were. His great fear was that if you would retire from the office of Provincial Minister, we would surely be called home. This thought made him suffer, and he was really miserable. I cannot begin to tell you all he does for us, if we were his own children he could not do more; to have us firmly established here seems the one aim of his life.

"On the 8th of November, the third anniversary of our coming here, he presented us with a 'Charter of Incorporation' of which he has sent you a copy by the last mail. . . .

"Now, my dear Father, I must acquaint you with some news. You are aware that up to the present time our work extended from Honolulu to Wailuku. In Honolulu we have one hundred leper patients under our care, and in the same yard we have the Kapiolani Home with thirteen girls aged from five to thirteen years, children of leper parents, who are not yet affected with the disease. In Wailuku we have a general Hospital, and a Girls' School, but you will remember that from the first it was expected that some of us would sooner or later go to Molokai to care for the suffering people there. The Board of Health hesitated to ask us to go because our number was too small, but lately it has become a serious question whether we should go.

"And on the 9th of February His Lordship the good Bishop called here, to speak about this serious question, and to ascertain how we felt about going. . . . I told him exactly how the Sisters felt, that they, or rather we, were not only willing but *anxious*, to go and care for the poor outcasts. He left with a light heart, and has since then held council with Mr. Gibson . . . now arrangements are being made for four Sisters to go to the leper settlement at Molokai. It may be two or three months before things will be ready, as a house will have to be built, and other arrangements made for the Sisters' comfort before Mr. Gibson will allow them to go. . . ."

This letter explains clearly the status of the Molokai problem with the Sisters at the date named. In the matter of incorporation, the charter in question is now in the archives of the order, and Walter Gibson's letter to Father Lesen, dated Feb. 12, 1887, is quoted at length in Appendix C.

Father Damien and Mr. Meyer, superintendent of the leper settlement, together searched for and settled upon a site for the Sisters' home on the fatal island. It is upon the crest of a little hill, some five minutes' walk from the church, and not far from the wharf at what is now Kalaupapa. The veranda commands an excellent view of the sea; the shock of incoming breakers and their spray almost make themselves felt in rough weather.

In spite of much literature about Molokai there are still many misunderstandings concerning it. It is a narrow island, roughly perhaps thirty-seven to thirty-eight miles long and eight wide, but the leper settlement which is toward one end, stands not on the real body of the island, but rather upon a short peninsula some three miles deep. At the base of this peninsula huge mountains called "pali" fence it across, cliffs of more than twenty-five hundred feet sheer fall, surmounted only with extreme difficulty and by a single path. Even in those days, though then they did not always have close supervision, the lepers did not rove about a great deal. Of course the terrain furnished one reason for this. The ground is stony and rough. The windward face of the island is a vast cliff. And at many points there large vessels may lie in close to shore in very deep water while overhead tower up tremendous escarpments, nearly a thousand feet high. Part of the island is used as pasturage for cattle, and there are some very good horses kept there for the patients to ride.

But as a whole Molokai is not easily accessible. The plain on which the leper settlement stood is barren and dusty and hot.

In the meanwhile affairs in the Branch Hospital grew better little by little, but troubles with the gamblers continued. In combating this difficulty, the Sisters to some extent derived aid from a native Hawaiian, Judge Kaluna, a man about forty, excellently educated, a good musician, the father of five children, a first-rate linguist, who had unusually good command of English. The career of Judge Kaluna offers curious and interesting first-hand evidence on the tremendous variety of folk to be found in the Branch Hospital.

The place continued to crowd to overflowing, and it became evident to all that a ship load would have to go to Molokai. Sisters and lepers alike dreaded this contingency, but Father Damien, during his recent visit, had made some efforts to break down the lepers' alarm. He pointed out that as long as the afflicted men remained in Honolulu they were amongst people who regarded them as unclean, that they found themselves shunned and disliked, that they were a burden to themselves and to all others, and that they must remain immured in a hospital which was first cousin to a prison. On Molokai, he said, you will be free; the immediate settlement will be yours, and for that matter much of the island. You can ride horses, go to valleys and mountain sides, gather fruit, and spend whole days in the ocean after shellfish and sea moss. The painting of this Hawaiian idyll restored the courage of some, though the gamblers generally remained intractable.

The day of fate came on, however, and when the steamer was ready to leave, the hospital inmates assembled at Mr. Gibson's orders, and heard the names of the men to be taken away called out. There is something very strange and terrible in this scene. I have watched soldiers who have just volunteered for duty that implied probable death; and the men assembled coolly, some laughing and joking, others stoical and methodical. But though their case was tragic, they had at least stepped into it with their eyes open, as the saying goes, and there was a chance, slender indeed, but still a chance, that they might come back. But, here, the parallel falters and fails. Lepers do not contract leprosy voluntarily, and the chances of the men bound for Molokai were *nil*. Lepers do not come back. These men were not leaving on an errand of valor, no bronze cross or bit of scarlet ribbon might lie at the end of their journey. They were pariahs.

The group gathered on the side veranda of the office facing the Convent. Most of the men who were told to pack their baggage were clever, intelligent young fellows, some of excellent family. Several carried guitars, and with good self-control, they fell into line, and began playing their plaintive native songs of farewell. With Molokai at a distance they had rebelled, but with Molokai only a day away, they faced their fate with all the coolness of the British soldiers who went down with the steamer *Birkenhead* while their band played.

The conveyances that carried off the lepers were not allowed to pass through Honolulu. So the victims went in small boats from a point on the beach not far from the Branch Hospital, and got on board when the steamer was already well out from the city. Judge Kaluna stood up in his skiff, as the sailors shoved off, and in a steady and commanding voice addressed the party left behind. He recounted briefly some of the disciplinary troubles in the Hospital, admitting his own faults, and urged the remainder to support the Hospital staff, and the regulations, with fidelity.

Then the oars dipped in the slow-swelling waves, the lepers with a curious unison played their "Aloha" on the native guitars, and the condemned men were on their way to their last stopping place. The Sisters were soon to follow.

Mother Marianne watched the departure with very mixed feelings, much depressed that any of her patients should be going from her, and to Molokai of all places, but not without a certain sense of relief. For it was not long before this that the same group of irreconcilables, headed by Judge Kaluna and Tom Burch, had formed a plot to kidnap Sister Benedicta and to kill Mother Marianne and the remaining Sisters. Mother Marianne had thwarted them very abruptly one day a few weeks earlier when in the course of a violent quarrel they endeavored to kill a native called Hiku. She had faced the whole group with an icy sternness when Hiku ran screaming to her for protection, and had broken the spirit of the attack. This was something the part-Hawaiians found it hard to forgive. That unflinching determination which accompanies intellectual convictions, and which the vacillating and irresolute half-native mind combats with difficulty, was particularly outstanding in

Mother Marianne, and while it explains the secret of her magnetic and tremendous power over the natives, it also gave rise to opposition. Small minds find it so difficult to forgive great minds their greatness. The plot, however, had been quelled as thoroughly as the impromptu plan to murder Hiku, and life had gone on as usual.

For a time after the departure there were only local plagues of a minor nature to annoy. One of the worst was rats. They were half as large as a cat, a light gray on the back with whiter belly and tail. They haunted the kitchens and dining room when the Hospital was first built, and the Sisters found them an insufferable nuisance. The likelihood that cats would aid in the spread of disease lessened their value to the Hospital, and the difficulty in keeping some of the ignorant and childlike inmates from eating poisoned food put out for rats, made poison less effective as a weapon. Indeed, one serious case of poisoning did occur when a gluttonous native woman took food intended for vermin, and in consequence of all these handicaps the battle against rats progressed slowly.

Then came a special committee of investigation from the legislature. But after visiting Kakaako and the Branch Hospital their report said, in part, "We wish to lay special stress upon the good offices of the

Franciscan Sisters—five in number—who have charge of the Hospital and Home. Their services are simply invaluable. All honor to whom honor is due."

In the meanwhile, work went on at Molokai. The Bishop Home for leper girls and women was under construction, and was presently completed. Like all these hospital and similar buildings, it was lightly constructed of wood, and planned and painted with a view to as thorough a cleaning and sterilization as at that time possible. Mother Marianne then decided it was the moment to visit Molokai personally, and to examine more directly into the nature of what was being accomplished.

But the Gibson ministry fell, there was violent political excitement in Honolulu for some days; Mr. Gibson, old, white-haired, and feeble, was mobbed in the street, and dragged about with a rope around his neck, and narrowly escaped lynching by hoodlum attackers. He had to go into exile, and a short time later died. Commenting upon his death Mother Marianne writes to her superior, May 5th, 1888:

"Indeed our loss is great. . . . It seemed that nothing gave him pleasure but to serve and wait on us. I have never in all my life seen a man like him. We miss him. He had great plans laid out—what all he was going to do for us, if

God had spared his life. God alone knows the *Why* of all the great trials and mean persecutions He allowed to come over this poor man."

The political uproar stopped all other activities for a time. Then Mother Marianne applied directly to the new president of the Board of Health, Doctor Emerson, for a permit to land on Molokai. Doctor Emerson expressed astonishment coupled with reluctance, but finally agreed, and even volunteered to accompany her. This kindness, however, did not advance him far in the opinion of the lepers, who, while admitting that he was a good man and a competent doctor, could not conceal their scornful amusement at his fears. "When he prepares medicine," one remarked, "he puts it on the gate post so we can get it without coming into his yard." This frame of mind is a curious contrast to that of his dauntless companion. Nevertheless, he was generally popular with the lepers, who laughed at him but liked him well.

On a gray unpleasant evening when wind and storm combined to presage ill, Doctor Emerson and Mother Marianne boarded the dirty little steamer *Lehua*, the only boat that ran regularly to the leper settlement. Mother Marianne's companion from the hospital was a little Portuguese girl called Olinda

Gomez, a good sailor, and thoroughly at home at sea. Subsequently, she entered the Order, taking the name of Sister Elizabeth.

They went aboard at about five o'clock. The wind became terrific; the boat danced like a leaf on the flood, the ocean quickly grew so rough that the whole party fled to cover. Even Olinda had her difficulties, and when a soaring wave threw the boat on her side, and Mother Marianne's glasses fell and slid across the deck, Olinda scrambled after them, but once on her hands and knees could not get back to a standing position till helped.

Father Damien's home for boys was three miles from the landing, but Mother Marianne found a wagon waiting to take them, and a group of excited lepers, an extraordinary *cortege*, as it were, to accompany them. Most of these men were lepers who had known her in the Branch Hospital, and who shed tears of joy at seeing her again. A curious conversation followed, in which the lepers explained their desire to remain near her as long as possible, and Mother Marianne replied by telling them that she would soon return to care for them, and not to leave them till death. She never referred to this conversation afterward, evidently looking upon her life and death on Molokai as a settled matter.

The Branch Hospital

The convent on the grounds at Bishop Home proved nicely furnished, and the carpenters just cleaning up. Mother Marianne inspected the whole provision, and returned to the boat. The wind which had lulled was rising again, and they had an angry sea to contend with. Doctor Emerson held his slicker over Olinda and Mother Marianne and protected them from the spray at the cost of a bad drenching for himself. The Hawaiian seamen with difficulty got their skiff to the steamer.

From Molokai Mother Marianne went on to Maui to inspect the work there. They reached Maui that evening, the sky cleared, and a full moon silvered the ocean, as tremendous writhing swells rolled up in slopes that seemed a quarter of a mile long, curled over at the crest in a lather of foam, and slowly sank away into a cavernous depth before rising again. The *Lehua* cast anchor far out, as it is always rough in the bay.

Again the party, this time minus Doctor Emerson, who was on his way back to Honolulu, went cautiously down the rope ladder into the ship's boat, and began their journey shoreward. Spray broke over them in showers, while Mother Marianne sat rigid and silent, and a male passenger facetiously advised Olinda to swallow this salty rain. They landed safely, and had that long seven-mile ride over rough, almost primeval, roads to Wailuku, where they arrived between nine and ten o'clock Thursday evening. They stayed in the Malulani Hospital till Saturday, then secured passage on the *Likelike* homeward.

The new convent at Bishop Home was a neat little one-story house painted white, with green blinds. It stood well back in a field at the top of a little hill. A six-foot veranda runs the whole length of the house, and a narrow corridor divides the building. A large parlor, two bedrooms, and a bath, open from the right, and from the left a smaller reception room, two bedrooms, and a small storeroom.

The Home was named for Mr. Gibson's friend, C. R. Bishop, who gave a very large donation so that the home in the settlement could be begun.

From the small reception room, a door opens to a dining room, and thence one emerges upon a rear veranda. Four small cottages were constructed nearby for the lepers, two for their sleeping quarters, one for cooking and meals, and one to be a receiving station for all surgical and medical work.

In concluding this chapter, it is worth while to remark that other folk beside Mother Marianne and Father Damien had previously had hopes of sending Sisters to Molokai. In regard to the contention, the following letter may well be quoted:

The Branch Hospital

DEPARTMENT OF INTERIOR

Honolulu, H. I.

May 22, 1888.

Sister Marianne,
Mother Superior, Franciscan Sisters,
Honolulu, H. I.

Dear Madam:

The fact is no doubt well known to you that one of the great hardships at the Molokai Leper settlement has been the lack of proper separate residences for single women and girls. This difficulty seems now in a fair way to be remedied so far as the necessary buildings are concerned, through the generous offer of the Hon. Charles R. Bishop to provide a home for women and girls, including a suitable residence for those who may have charge of the same.

But such a house will not accomplish its end unless it is well ordered and governed. From the self-sacrificing example of yourself and the other Sisters of your order who are now ministering to the lepers, the Government has been led to hope that others of your order might be willing to assume the charge of such a Home.

The duties to be discharged are of such a nature that I do not feel that I have the right to urge the matter upon you—or even to ask that any woman should devote herself to such a work.

I will therefore confine myself to saying that the construction of such a Home will immediately be proceeded with, to be ready for occupation in, say, three or four months from now. The number of women and girls who will occupy the Home cannot be definitely estimated, but it will probably be in the vicinity of one hundred, with a possible increase to one hundred and fifty. The number of Sisters who would be needed in connection therewith is a matter which you are more competent to decide than I am, but it seems to me that six or eight would perhaps be a proper number.

If there are any of the members of your order, or of other orders having similar objects, who would be willing to undertake the charge of the proposed Home, the Hawaiian government will thankfully accept their assistance, and will do all in its power to aid and assist them, and in every possible way ameliorate the discomforts and difficulties of their position.

Any information which you may be pleased to give me concerning the likelihood of obtaining sisters for this work will be deeply appreciated,

by your humble servant,
(signed) L. Thurston,
Minister of the Interior.

It is pretty well evident that the deeply lasting value of the Franciscan Sisters' work was now thoroughly clear, even in circles far removed from the religious life, and whose main interests were not at all religious, rather purely and solely political.

V

MOLOKAI AHINA

On Tuesday, November 13, 1888, the Sisters who were to go to Molokai assembled; Mother Marianne Kopp, Sister Vincent McCormick, and Sister Leopoldina Burns. The doctors and some of their friends gathered at the hospital to bid them a restrained adieu. Reverend Father Mathias accompanied them as a temporary chaplain. It was a gloomy gray unpleasant evening. They left at five o'clock, and went aboard the *Lehua*. The wind was rising, and whistling mournfully, as it sped out of the vast empty spaces of the Pacific, and apparently a storm threatened. Twenty women and girls, confirmed cases shipped by the Board of Health, accompanied the Sisters. A few male lepers added to the account. The stars were dim in a drift of scud that blew and blew uneasily before the wind. Rain began to fall at about eleven o'clock, with the sea growing steadily rougher. All the Sisters remained on deck, wrapped up as well as possible, and facing the weather rather than to go below into the warm wet stifling atmosphere of the cabins, though later the sky cleared and there was moonlight.

Nor could their companions have added much to the tone of the journey. Sorrow, dejection, and exile awaited the lepers. It was physically possible indeed for the Sisters at any time to leave Molokai, and their case was not unbearable, but for the twenty companions death furnished the sole source of escape. No tragedy could be pitched on a gloomier note than theirs. The disfigured faces and gnarled halting limbs were as strange as anything Dante saw in the wood of living men. And as she reeled through the night and storm toward Kalaupapa, the vessel seemed freighted with unearthly beings from some strange impossible existence, spirits from a distant planet passing through this world on their way to another.

The general supposition was that the Sisters were to remain reasonably cheerful amid these surroundings, and do what they could to keep up the spirits of their charges. But photographs of the boatloads of people who used to go to Molokai tell their own story. It beggars description. Comment is useless.

At last the *Lehua* passed into the shadow of land, an enormous black shadow projecting from equally enormous cliffs along shore, and from the gigantic pali on the island itself. A little red speck that seemed to lie at the foot of one of the highest crags appeared, the light at Kalaupapa. Then a gray band lightened in the eastern sky, the cloud blew away, and a series of white streaks of light came up, then a scarlet flash, and it was day.

There before them lay Molokai Ahina. Gray Molokai as the Hawaiians said, the enigmatic island so variously described by various observers from R. L. Stevenson to Katharine Fullerton Gerould. To some its wild beauty is repellent, to others its nakedness, aridity, and loneliness destroy all trace of charm, and to still others the presence of the merciless destroyer evokes a shudder, and in the face of leprosy they can think of nothing else.

It is an angular land, probably once entirely volcanic, and it still has huge crags of blackish lava rock. In some valleys, not near the leper settlement, however, there is rank vegetation, and many horses and cattle feed, but its most noteworthy characteristic as one approaches by sea is the jutting cliffs that belt the island around, so that in most places it is impossible to land.

The sun is brilliant as a fine spun golden vapor, and this great sea-encircled rock is forever fringed with spray as the ocean drives against the bases of the bluffs, like a succession of battering rams. Remember that at most points there is practically no beach, the vertical cliffs continue almost straight down below the surface, and within baseball throw of shore are some immense "deeps." With no shelving slope to act as a brake and to delay their approach, the great rollers that rise out of the Pacific assault the island like an express train at full speed, and the shock and roar of their collision with the flat-faced, iron-hard lava crags is worthy of Dante's pen. Hence, the mighty geysers of spray, hence the misty fog that so often veils lower parts of the shore, hence the gorgeous rainbows in the wind and sunshine. It is a view of sinister beauty.

High on the windy peaks the palms wave in the breeze like feathery fans, here and there cascades dash over the rim and resemble long white stalactites scattered to thin mist in their tremendous drop, and the sea gulls with long sweeps of the wing dive screaming through their airy world, or float as if enchanted and motionless in the blue. The very landscape seems to induce that mild melancholy and passive resignation so common in the brown islanders. It is as if yesterday, today, and tomorrow, are all one. The perception of time is blunted if not annhiliated. The nervous occidental falls under a strange lethargic spell. In the warm South Seas it is, in a sense, always summer. Seasons change, the tireless trade winds blow, new flowers and fruits appear, sweet, rich, many colored, but that dreaming motionless sea-scape is ever the same; the same gales blow, the same tides crash in white on the rocks, and the scene seems to say that life and death come and go but Molokai and the sea abide forever. In the presence of such immense natural forces, the human being is dwarfed and impotent.

The vessel came up to shore more easily than anyone had anticipated, and the party went down the rope ladder, a little after five o'clock, November 14, just with the coming of dawn, and were met at the wharf by a number of parishioners, with Father Damien arriving a little later. The leper women and girls who had landed before the Sisters were delighted to welcome their friends. The chapel was only about one hundred yards from shore, and the other buildings not far.

Some of the visitors' troubles began almost at once. No well had been dug, there was no reservoir, and the only water available was a supply of rain water run off newly shingled roofs and brown as coffee. A few cocoanut trees whistled in the lonely wind, a baking sun beat down upon the clearing, then the silence of utter desolation rested upon the settlement.

The authorities had originally set the date of the Sisters' departure for Molokai on Monday, November 12, 1888. But at the last moment news arrived that a violent storm and heavy freshet had destroyed the waterworks at the head, that is, the reservoir and part of the pipes were swept away. It was a serious blow. There was no good water, and to supply the Sisters' projected convent and hospital, the Hawaiian government was bringing the water from a clean pure stream nearly five miles distant. To effect this it had been necessary to build a reservoir and to lay down a great deal of pipe.

The Board of Health held a hasty meeting on Monday, November 12, to decide if it was advisable for the Sisters to leave Honolulu. It was finally voted that they should go on to Molokai at once, that an engineer and mechanics should also go immediately to repair the damages, and that some large casks should be shipped so that water could be carted to the settlement.

The Sisters themselves referred to this new establishment as the St. Elizabeth Convent, but it is generally known as the Bishop Home, because, as already explained, much of the money expended here was personally donated by Mr. C. R. Bishop, a wealthy banker of Honolulu.

Father Wendelin Moeller came to the Kalaupapa station six days after the Sisters. He had charge of the church at Kalaupapa, and Fathers Damien and Conrardy took care of the work at Kalawao. Father Damien came repeatedly to Kalaupapa to visit, but refused to enter the buildings, preferring generally to remain at a little distance while he talked. He was already far advanced, and failing rapidly. There was death written on his face.

Mother Marianne was very anxious to inspect the boys' home, and to find wherein it might differ from her own establishment. Father Damien sent a little wagon to convey the Sisters, and all three went. It was not an exhilarating ride. The horse could not take them faster than a walk, the ill-kept road was excessively rough with large stones and occasional deep holes. They passed various little lonely clearings in which desolate cabins stood, all alike in grisly silence, hot and motionless under a tropic sun, but not once did they see the inmates. Lepers who lived in these ruinous places shrank away from notice like frightened deer.

The observant cavalcade viewed the old extinct volcano, and coming to a long hill looked down and saw at its foot some broad green fields covering half a square mile, near them at the foot Father Damien's own church, and the roughly built shanties that housed many lepers, and halfway up the slope a little Protestant church.

The Sisters could hardly refrain from laughter at sight of Father Damien's church; for to please the æsthetic senses of his native parishioners he had

[83]

painted it with all the gay colors he could find, and to Sister Leopoldina it resembled a Chinese shop. But the poor natives were profoundly pleased, so Father Damien was, too.

Around his church in true continental fashion were grouped the graves of his dead parishioners, and the pastor having received in the arrival of the Sisters what he practically regarded as his "Nunc dimittis," was already looking forward to the day when he, too, would sleep among the lepers' graves. He was then engaged in the construction of a new church only partly finished. Much of the masonry he had himself completed, though his swollen hands now made such work a torture. He had constructed a large concrete bake-oven in the adjacent yard, near a cook shack; and some of the leper boys, with a forethought that was not without its humor, used the top of the bake-oven for a bed in chilly weather.

There were over one hundred boys and men in this settlement, the majority of them well-advanced cases. Those active enough to get about busied themselves as best they could, Damien doing everything in his power to combat the mental lethargy that besets so many victims.

He gave the Sisters a glad welcome to his miserable abode, and showed them what improvements he had effected. Standing there and looking over the

wretched surroundings, one was impelled to an overwhelming sense of sorrow, a poignant feeling, hard
to analyze, hard to understand. Perhaps this divine
sorrow was what Vergil had in mind when he wrote
"Tears are for human things," but Vergil was thinking of strong healthy people, not of an impulsive
Belgian boy who had given away his life in this
heathen wilderness. It was a depressing scene and
nearly reduced the visitors to actual tears, but it made
deep impressions upon all. Mother Marianne seemed
glad she had come; she knew well now what she had
to face.

It must always be remembered, in estimating the
work both of Father Damien and of Mother
Marianne, that they cared for only such lepers as
would accept their ministrations. Many lepers who
disliked Father Damien, either because he endeavored to curb their licentious habits, or because of his
faith, or because restrictions irked them, never came
near the Kalawao settlement where he presided.
Similarly, when the Sisters provided a refuge for
leprous women and girls at Kalaupapa, many did not
avail themselves of the aid afforded.

A curious incident occurred in connection with the
Sisters' first visit to Kalawao. Father Damien in a
desperate effort to show hospitality in this hideous
place, had had a small meal prepared, and he wanted

the Sisters to sit down and eat. Mother Marianne had given orders that no Sister should do this (Father Damien's cook was leprous, and leprosy probably lurked in many points in his abode), but Mother Marianne had gone with Mr. Dutton to inspect some distant work, and the unhappy host was insistent. He even informed them that he had had the meal specially prepared by a non-leper.

So Sisters Vincent and Leopoldina yielded to his importunate urging, sat down at the lepers' table, and ate a little of the food. They had told Father Damien of their Superior's requirement, but in his impulsive way he overrode objections and half commanded them to eat. They were in great mental distress, and could hardly have enjoyed their food. They dreaded to offend the poor sufferer who was then on the verge of the grave, and equally they dreaded the rebuke of their superior.

On the way home to Kalaupapa that evening they confessed to Mother Marianne. She in turn was much disturbed, and for a moment hesitated to speak. But, finally, she reminded her helpers that orders are orders, and with this brief admonition would have let the matter drop, for she saw how upset they also were. But it did not end there.

Father Damien was likewise thinking of the same thing, and as the night wore on, grew more and more worried, considering that he had been the occasion of the two women transgressing an order. He could not sleep well.

Mother Marianne felt some astonishment when told at an early hour next morning that Father Damien wanted to see her, but speech failed her when the unhappy man coming up to her, fell on his knees before her and began to beg for forgiveness because he had urged the two Sisters to eat in his house. It was with difficulty that she reassured him. That downright and undeviating honesty which distinguished Damien from boyhood, and his sensitive concern over the slightest shadow of an unfairness never flashed out more clearly than in this instance.

In a letter dated May 16, 1889, addressed to the Bishop of Olba, Mother Marianne describes her first visit to the Boys' Home, which she says occurred on November 28, 1888, thus, a fortnight after her arrival. "Ever since that day, my heart has bled for them, and I was anxious and hungry to help to put a little more sunshine into their dreary lives."

Now began for the three Sisters the long and wearisome task of organizing their resources and putting their receiving station in order, the same work that had so long burdened them in the Branch Hospital at Honolulu. Amongst the many victims the Sisters found numbers who had formerly been in this same Branch Hospital and who recalled their stay with pleasure.

On December 8, 1888, in a letter to her superior in Syracuse, she writes:

"Here I am at the Leper Settlement on the island of Molokai to which place we, Sisters Leopoldina, Vincent, and myself, came on the 14th of November. And here it was that I spent the 19th, the twenty-fifth anniversary of my profession." [Referring to her entry into the order.]

Her thoughts must, unquestionably, have been strange and varied ones on that day, as she reviewed the twenty-five years that had fleeted by while she served God to the best of her ability, and labored for her afflicted brethren. The life of the little emigrant girl, now more than half spent, had traveled a wonderful course from the cool, green valleys of Hesse to this wild, barren peak in the south Pacific.

Her thoughts that day could have reviewed an incomparable cycle; from the cheerful German home of her babyhood, well known through the descriptions of her parents; the craggy little mountains, the old, old roads, the quaint villages, sandy pine forests, balsamic and sweet, and the chilly springs and streams in which, according to Heinrich Heine's fancy, Ilse the fairy plays. Perhaps she recalled, certainly she must have read, the hapless poet's verses.

Molokai Ahina

Ich bin die Prinzessin Ilse, Ich wohne im Ilsenstein,
Kom' mit nach meinem Schlosse, wir wollen selig sein.

But the kaleidoscope has changed. The crystal ball
of memory shows the north Atlantic, stormy, glitter-
ing, and green, its surface a-glisten, and high winds
tossing its spray. Then, America, and adventures in
a new strange land; youth rapidly verging into young
womanhood, associations shifting and changing like
the lights that sparkle and play in a rapid stream on
a summer's day; then the Sisterhood, service; life devoted to charity; now, once more the ocean, this time
the Pacific, vast, turbulent, seemingly illimitable;
and now in the midst of this heaving restless blue
plain, a lonely arid reddish rock swept by wild winds
that sprang as it were out of nowhere.

And memory conjures up Napoleon on the cliffs
at Saint Helena. But unlike the desperate Corsican,
this great soul had come voluntarily to her last destination. The sand in Mother Marianne's glass was
more than half run out, but as she pondered upon the
thin swift stream, whatever she *may* have thought,
one thing we know she *did* think. To resume the
letter quoted above:

"I was happy to do something in honor of the dear saint
(Elizabeth) on whose feast twenty-five years ago I have
received so many and great graces.

"Accept, dear Mother, my heartfelt thanks for all you have done for me—many many years ago, I believe only for your kind influence I would not have been received into the order. So if I have done a little good during these years that have passed into eternity you share the reward of it."

Comment would be impertinent. But if any doubter wonders whether she propounded to herself the question, "Has it been worth while—all this sacrifice, effort, and pain?" and what the answer was, I think we can reconstruct the answer from her life, her letters, even from the remarks quoted above; it would have been a clear and unhesitating "Yes."

VI

FATHER DAMIEN'S DEATH

ALTHOUGH the settlement never has snow or frost, there are often in winter very cold, unpleasant, dark days; frequently accompanied by rain and wind, and a furious and tumultuous sea. On such a day, toward the end of January, 1889, Father Damien came to the Bishop Home upon what eventually proved his last visit. He was then extremely sick, his face and lips deathly gray, spotted with red inflamed tubercles, and burning with fever. His voice had become very low and husky, hardly more than a whisper. He would not, of course, enter the house, and he sat by the corner of the veranda, and talked to Mother Marianne.

His main concern, now, he told her, was that she and her Sisters should come to see his little church, which he had nearly finished. He remained but a short while, for the disease was torturing him, and he could hardly keep quiet. The wind was up, and a fine rain came driving in over the misty dark sea. It was the only time he ever came without visiting the lepers in every cottage. They had loved his cheerful manner, and looked forward with delight to his every coming, and now that he failed to meet them, they read a dim foreboding in the event.

The next day the wagon came for Mother Marianne and the Sisters, and again the party went creeping over the rocky, ill-kept road. Father Damien and Brother Dutton met them. Father Damien showed the new church to Sister Leopoldina while Brother Dutton talked to Mother Marianne. Father Damien was happy as a child. He said, "I have finished the work our divine Lord has given me to do, and I am ready now to go. I had such poor help that I had to do nearly all of it with these poor hands." He glanced at the disfigured joints. His hands were then dreadfully swollen, the fingers nearly shapeless. He laughed and went on, "Only think how good our divine Lord is! I begged Him to send someone to take my place, and He has sent two priests, the good Mother, and her Sisters, and with Mr. Dutton to assist them, and this is my crowning gift, to be able to finish my church."

He then continued to explain to the Sisters that a Mr. Baldwin, a wealthy sugar planter on Maui, would build a very good Home for the boys and men; and Mother Marianne could have the Home placed wherever she liked, and the Sisters would have charge of it. "When I think," he concluded, "my poor afflicted children will have a mother's care, I am happy indeed! The poor children have been so neglected. I could not fill a mother's place."

After spending some three to four hours at the settlement, the Sisters returned home. They were very silent on the way back. Mother Marianne was thinking of the boisterous and unruly groups she would have to deal with, and sometimes to direct, men who had little knowledge of order, and less desire for it; and some of whom looked upon law only as a tyrant that had condemned them to a living death upon Molokai.

But ever and anon, as sudden lightning flashes pierce a stormy landscape deep at night, one's thoughts darted back to that simple young priest, son of a Belgian citizen, and heir to all the traditions of a civilized and cultured land, who had so generously given himself, his life, and his prospects, for the benefit of a wild, sometimes illiterate group, such as Kipling called "half savage and half child." Surely no one bore "The White Man's Burden" more appropriately than Father Damien de Veuster. Buried alive in this lonely barren place for sixteen years, during a part of this time without a companion, except the unfortunate outcasts that he cared for; with rarely a civilized voice to shatter the enveloping solitude; with the distant muttering of the ocean drumming ceaselessly against the iron-hard cliffs of the island; madness must have waited upon him, had he not walked incessantly in the presence of his God.

An English artist called Clifford, an exceedingly intelligent and cultured man, had come to sketch and to get acquainted with Father Damien, and for other reasons. He spent much of his time with the dying priest. Mr. Clifford was particularly generous in his care of the sick, and his efforts to instruct them were edifying, while it was partly through his work that the British government later erected the beautiful memorial to Father Damien.

Brother James, a Christian Brother from Australia, came a little later, to aid in nursing Father Damien. A tall Irishman, handsome in his younger days, now thin and ascetic, he added his efforts to those of Brother Dutton.

Though Father Damien suffered greatly he did not remain in bed till near the closing days of March, when it became clear to all that the end was not far. Father Wendelin asked him if there were any particular place in which he would like to be buried.

"Yes," he said. "I would like to rest by the side of my church, under the good old lauhala tree where

I rested so many nights before I had any other shelter."

Father Wendelin told him they would prepare his tomb there; so that he could rest in his old favorite place.

He laughed, and said, "It has always been my wish."

On the day before he died, Mother Marianne and Sister Vincent went to see him, to say farewell and to ask his blessing. Mr. Dutton, Brother James, and Father Conrardy were with him, and were endeavoring to keep him as comfortable as possible. He was weak, and spoke to them in a whisper, but said he was very happy.

On the following morning, April 15, 1889, at about eight o'clock, in perfect quiet, he passed peacefully to the presence of his God Whom he had served so long and so faithfully.

Mother Marianne and Sister Leopoldina went at once, and assisted in the plans for the funeral, and the preparation of his casket. They found plenty to do, for now that the shepherd had been stricken, most of his flock seemed dazed by grief and despondency. Only the white men retained their energy and continued at their tasks.

A brilliant sun, a cool fresh breeze from the mountain, made the morning of the funeral more cheerful. Mother Marianne gathered a procession of the leper women and girls to attend the ceremony; the natives in their white dresses with black sashes and white hats. It was all very poor, but derived a solemnity from circumstances not usually associated with earthly grandeur. Father Wendelin celebrated the Mass, and delivered the funeral address in Hawaiian, and the body was lowered into a concrete vault beside the church and under the old tree.

Father Damien's work had ended, and Mother Marianne had now much of it to carry on. In a letter dated May 6, 1889, to her superior in Syracuse, she writes:

"I did not intend to let you wait so long for a letter, but time slips so rapidly from me that I cannot accomplish all I would. So kindly accept the good will for the deed. Often I think and speak of you, and the dear Sisters with you, and as often make attempts to write, only to fail in doing so. We are only three Sisters here, and all three have our hands full from early morning till late at night. . . .

"Our dear Father Damien died on the 15th of April. His place of residence is three miles from Kalaupapa where we live. We visited him before he died. And standing at his bedside one could imagine hearing the Voice of God calling him to come to his reward. His was a grand and noble life of self-sacrifice, how closely he followed in the footsteps of our loving Saviour, living and dying for the poor outcasts. What more can a poor mortal do than give his life for his fellow creatures. . . ."

Father Damien's Death

After Father Damien's death there was great confusion in the labors at the settlement. To complicate
matters there were many changes in officialdom at
Honolulu. The Board of Health had the old Receiving Station, at the Branch Hospital of Kakaako,
where the Sisters had first labored, broken up, and removed to a location some miles down the beach. It was
hidden away in a beautiful grove of algaroba trees,
and in general it seems that the removal was a benefit
to the locality, for the old place had been a very un-
sightly spot, and without doubt had done nothing to
advertise Honolulu. The new location, so far removed, gave better service in many respects, yet had
its disadvantages as well. The lepers complained of
the terrific heat, and of course once the Receiving
Station went to pieces, the Sisters had other and new
tasks.

There was, too, the matter of the Kapiolani Home,
and of the wild little leper children, some now well
grown, who still had to be cared for. The years have
a way of moving on, and they bring irretrievable
changes. Mother Marianne was asked to approve this
and that alteration, and was busied by correspondence, without ceasing.

A number of the buildings in the leper settlement
at Molokai were put up very rapidly. This was the
more easily understood as one remembers that when

the old Receiving Station at Honolulu was broken up, some of the buildings were torn to pieces, and the sections shipped to Molokai, where a group of carpenters were given the job of reassembling the parts and making new houses. Not a very difficult task, but one that solved the housing problem more quickly than thoroughly. Of course this was long before the days in which the United States became a dominant factor in Hawaiian affairs, and the native government was at once dilatory, ill-informed, and alternately extravagant and parsimonious in its expenditures. The authorities, I think, were always sincerely anxious to help, but they did not always show good judgment in the methods employed, or the way in which they went about their tasks.

Perhaps it was believed that Mother Marianne should be well pleased with hasty buildings full of nail holes, without paint or putty to cover the crevices, and very uncertain methods of heating. Whatever she thought about the matter though, she kept to herself. She, indeed, remained extremely sparing of her criticisms, preferring few words as a rule, and directly to the point. There is no complaining spirit in her correspondence and papers; and the patience and skill with which she adapted herself to prescribed conditions, and made the best of her meager resources, would be a continual marvel, were the explanation not ready to hand in the simple fact of her presence upon Molokai. Her faith knew no bounds. Sister Leopoldina, worried by alarmist doctors, once spoke about the danger of contracting leprosy. It was a concrete problem to her who had most of the work of dressing the lepers' sores. One day she said casually to Mother Marianne, "Mother, what will you do with me if I become a leper?"

"You will never become a leper," was the quick reply. "I know we are all exposed, and I know, too, that God has called us for this work. If we are prudent, and do our duty, He will protect us. Do not allow it to trouble you, and when the thought comes to you, drive it from your mind. And, remember, you will never be a leper, nor will any Sister of our Order."

VII

ROBERT LOUIS STEVENSON

On May 9, 1889, Sister Crescentia and Sister Irene came to Molokai from Honolulu to join the field of labor. As they were leaving Honolulu they met Bishop Herman and Father Leonor, who had come to the wharf to say good-by to a visitor then starting for Molokai. They had a stormy trip. As usual there was high wind and rain, and the sea fairly boiled under the downpour. The Sisters were depressed, and one of them cried. They thought it remarkable that the strange traveler who accompanied them seemed as depressed as themselves, and once shed tears, but naturally they had nothing to say to him.

He landed alone and early before any one else had disembarked. There was no one at hand to welcome him officially, which perhaps suited this man as well, since it gave him an opportunity to investigate in person. He walked by himself to the doctor's home, which was at least two and a half miles from the landing, a lonely dreary walk in the gray of dawn. The wind blew wild and hard, and a thin mist flew in the air, recalling possibly some days in his faraway Highlands.

Stevenson was then in poor health, with his face very pale, and its natural thinness somewhat sharply accentuated. He chatted with the few he met on the road who could speak English. To say he aroused interest amongst the lepers would be putting it mildly.

Next morning at about ten o'clock Sister Leopoldina, on an errand among the sick, saw a strange man standing at the fence. He was quite white, and locks of shining black hair drooped across his broad forehead now beaded with perspiration. He had remarkable eyes, sunken, with dark rings around them, but alight with an extraordinary fire of intelligence. Not a large man, and dressed in gray, he had a bright, red-silk sash tied around his waist, and hanging down in a tassel at one side, native fashion. Sister Leopoldina walked over to the fence to ask what he wanted, and noted his remarkably long, bony fingers, clasping his hat. They were the sensitive fingers of an artist.

She asked, "Is there anything I can do for you?"

"Oh," he said, "I was just admiring your cheerful home. It is the only pleasant place I find in the settlement. I would like to see the Reverend Mother, if I am not too early."

Sister Leopoldina, who had no suspicion of his identity, led him into the yard, and directed him how to find the Superior.

He provided a new croquet set for the feeble leper children, and next day, despite Mother Marianne's protests, proceeded to teach the victims the game. The Hawaiians could hardly believe a healthy white man would turn aside to notice them, or would not shun them as did all others. He expended three hours with the excited children, and when he had ended had not only taught them to play but had made firm friends of all. He learned most of their names, and nearly exhausted himself in his efforts.

Mother Marianne came up to him and said in her gentle way, "It is not right for you to exert yourself. It may be dangerous, in your condition."

Stevenson smiled and answered, "Mother, you have some very clever young ladies. If I am not mistaken, Waikahi will know the game better than I before the end of my visit. I have had a very pleasant morning, and will be here tomorrow afternoon."

He ate lunch, and chatted with Mother Marianne for an hour, a conversation that drifted far from Molokai, and crossed half a world. But when he came next day at two o'clock, the children were ready with a joyful and noisy welcome. Mother Marianne met him in the yard, and begged him not to start the game, or at least to wait for a while, but all the time he was listening to her his restless eyes were following the little lepers, and at last he rushed off to join them. He put such life and excitement into the amusement that time passed all too quickly. He took off his hat and coat, and worked so hard at the play that from time to time he would throw himself on the soft grass to rest until summoned to go on. Near five o'clock they gave up, everyone tired and happy.

Stevenson was so pale and his breathing so quick that Mother Marianne became desperately alarmed. "What could we do?" she asked the other Sisters, "should he have a hemorrhage in this dreadful place? Where he could not have proper medicine, food, or care. He is not thinking of himself, but he is determined those girls must know how to play before he leaves them!"

Indeed, he succeeded so well that the whole group of patients learned to play.

He told Mother Marianne he could not bear to say good-by to the rest, and, when he left, delegated to her the task of greeting the others for him. The delight these simple little souls found in his company was only equalled by their despair when they discovered he had gone. But on the following Thursday when the steamer came from Honolulu, the children of the colony were astounded to find he had sent a five-hundred-dollar piano for the lepers of Bishop Home.

"As for the girls in the Bishop Home," Stevenson afterward wrote, "of the many beautiful things I have been privileged to see in life, they, and what has been done for them, are not the least beautiful. When I came there first the Sisters and the majority of the boarders were gone up the hill upon a weekly treat, guava hunting, and only Mother Marianne and the specially sick were left at home. I was told things which I heard with tears, of which I sometimes think at night, and which I spare the reader, I was shown the sufferers then at home; one, I remember, white with pain, the tears standing in her eyes. But, thank God, pain is not the rule in this revolting malady; and the general impression of the home was one of cheerfulness, cleanliness, and comfort. The dormitories were airy, the beds neatly made; at every bedhead was a trophy of Christmas cards, pictures, and photographs, some framed with shells, and all arranged with care and taste."

Stevenson showed perhaps his keenest insight into the nature of work amongst lepers by the very fact that he came every day while at the island to see Mother Marianne, and to discuss with her what she was doing. It is an interesting commentary upon her intellectual power as well as her saintly character, that she exerted such remarkable influence over this restless genius, but even at the ends of the earth when two shrewd minds meet, they know each other. There is a certain dry, matter-of-factness in the strictly scientific attitude toward disease that is redolent of professional cleanliness and germicide; correct but not entirely human. But to an intelligent woman who devoted her life to such terrible work because a very human person died upon a cross for her, the side of humanity could not fail to have immense importance. And while not slow to recognize what science has done, and it is much, Mother Marianne grasped with all the clarity of Antigone herself the import of the spiritual appeal. *"Man does not live by bread alone."*

Human things have the deepest values. Men will die for an idea, but they will not die for a test tube. In action, in 1918, near a little French village called Gesnes, I watched an American soldier deliberately offer himself as a target for German machine gunners so that his fellow soldiers could better sight their own guns, and was glad beyond words when he got off unscratched. But if the incident proved anything, it proved what was just mentioned; the human aspect, the will to help, the voluntary sacrifice, is the important thing. "If you have faith sufficient to move mountains," once wrote Saint Paul, "and have not charity it will avail you nothing." The greatest saints are the men like Thomas Aquinas and Peter Claver who *do* good. Judged by this standard, Mother Marianne's status is not hard to determine.

Out of her heritage of faith and study, charity and reflection, experience and suffering, she evolved what we might call her philosophy of life, and Robert Louis Stevenson, that cunning psychologist and seldom rivaled artist, found it fascinating to hear. It was not only what she said, for her words were few, but the very intonation, the outlook expressed, and even more important, the outlook implied, told volumes.

We live, each of us, in two worlds, one shallow and easily communicated, readily recognized by all; the other deeper, of vaster import, a strange country into which we draw back less often, a field never clearly revealed to anyone and sometimes not well known even to its possessor. The way in which we "feel" about many of the most serious things in life is more weighty than any number of commands and covenants. When a boy does not wish to cheat a companion in a game, because he instinctively "feels" that this would not be "fair" he is far more likely to prove dependable for fundamental honesty than the boy who quotes the law against cheating and is governed solely by rule and regulation.

Hence the basic importance of that spiritual background out of which our deepest decisions and truest feelings come. And with Mother Marianne the spiritual element was the very factor upon which all her life and sacrifice hinged. No wonder, then, in that distant island, condemned to die far from his native soil, amongst savages and half-castes, in a land strange as a primeval world, the redoubtable Robert Louis Stevenson found conversation with this brilliant woman interesting and good.

VIII

THE STORMS OF MOLOKAI

NOT many days after Mother Marianne first came to the leper island for residence, an incident developed that may be worth relation, both as illustrating the native frame of mind and the possibilities of weather in this otherwise peaceful scene. The visitors had noticed the ruins of a building that at one time might have been very beautiful; tall stone walls, but no windows or doors, only ragged fissures where openings of more orderly nature should have existed, and the roof entirely destroyed.

One day Sister Leopoldina put the question directly to an aged Hawaiian woman who knew a little English: "Were these ruins at one time the home of Chiefs, or royal people?"

"Oh, no, Sister," said the aged crone, in substance, "it is not that long ago. Ten years ago it was a beautiful Calvinist church. It had a very high tower, and a lovely sweet-sounding bell. But every ten years we have frightful whirlwinds, in the native we call it 'devil wind,' because it sweeps things away, and ten years ago it was so very strong that it did many strange and ghostly things; it took away the whole top of that church and left the ruins that you see. The people heard their lovely bell ringing as it went, and it has never been seen nor heard of since. Not a scrap of wood was left from the roof."

The Sisters smiled, and their smile must have conveyed a scepticism that was recognizable, for the old woman resumed: "The people think it was carried away by the spirits of the old Chiefs, and there are many places in this settlement that are forbidden (taboo), and should anyone build on these forbidden places, trouble is sure to come to him. When they built their church they did not know it is a forbidden place. Every ten years we must expect this frightful whirlwind, and it would be no use repairing the church, as it would be destroyed again. And perhaps something more frightful would happen to them. The whirlwind will visit us again this year, as it is ten years since the last great storm. When it is coming, you can hear it howling like wild animals."

As this conversation took place, it was not many generations since these same old Chiefs referred to had waged furious war in the pleasant vales, and celebrated hideously after victory. And even then the power of taboo was so strong that a native who thought he had offended the evil spirits could sicken and die in a matter of hours.

So no more was said at the moment, but one afternoon, later, two Sisters had to go out from the hospital on a sudden accident case. It was a brilliant day, with a glaring coppery sun in an unclouded sky, and over the broad stones heat waves shimmered and danced. At about three o'clock, although no breeze blew in the fields, and the green lush vegetation in some spots lay stagnant and heavy, a little wind began to move upon the open road. Clouds of fine red dust quickly mounted into the upper air, as if churned up by the feet of many invisible marching men. A poet might fancy the spirits of some of the grim old island Chiefs were returning.

An hour later the Sisters had finished their errand, and were going back to the Home. No sign of anything unusual prevailed, but before they reached their destination they discovered that the little heat whirlwinds, now greatly augmented in height and velocity, had quitted the leper peninsula and moved out over the ocean. For some time this strange phenomenon continued, the spiralling wind playing beautifully upon the smooth surface of the sea. It lifted great patches of water, whirling it in circles, as it had done with the dust of the road, carrying it high in air and scattering it with such force that no one could see where it fell. All this it accomplished in quiet, but with a precision and force that had in them something malignant.

The leper children gathered in knots in the yard to witness this strange apparition on the blue water, for indeed there is an excellent view of the sea from the grounds, and they enjoyed it with great glee. Some of them constructed little paper balloons, and sent them aloft. These tiny projectiles sped away with a swiftness that betokened enormous suction bearing down from above, and to experienced observers carried an alarming hint. By this time the whole atmosphere was beginning to experience a strange agitation, and the usual sultry heat seemed peculiarly intensified in spite of the restless little air currents that continued to whirl and pirouette.

Mother Marianne felt some alarm as evening came on, but endeavored to keep everything in its wonted tranquil routine. The sun set red and angry, while the ocean at the skyline seemed to rise up like a distant wall to meet it, and the rapid tropic dusk began to gather a little earlier that night than usual. The deep now showed signs of uneasy agitation, the waters tossing and lifting straight up in a manner not at all common to the more customary forms of the great typhoons.

Then the people of the settlement sat down by

lamplight to a supper they were not destined to finish. In the flickering yellow glow of the old lamps their faces reflected grotesquely the uncertain forebodings that disturbed all. There was an uneasy period of a few minutes, during which atmospheric pressure behaved strangely, alternately bearing down and relaxing, as if the settlement were from time to time in the center of a great vacuum, then in turn subjected to an immense weight of air.

Suddenly the light breeze swelled till it became terrific. And, strangely enough, it carried the peculiar sound to which the old Hawaiian woman had referred, a voice like the howling of animals in pain. Its uproar was so gigantic as to drown even the abrupt roaring outcry of the sea.

Mother Marianne said, "Come! We must go to the children."

The lepers gathered quickly, rushing like mad through the thick dark, shrieking and screaming as if the day of doom had come. Then, almost instantly, the moon rose, brilliant and terrible, in an unclouded sky, and the hurricane came suddenly to its peak. All the loose débris in the settlement whirled away, boards, pails, barrels, cans, rolling and bounding; some of the wreckage lifted bodily into the air and swept away to sea.

The native children, terrified little animals now,

crouched down flat in hollows, without speaking a word. The Sisters got all the girls into one of the cottages that was firmly built of strong new lumber, avoiding the other ragged buildings made of cast-off materials shipped from Honolulu. With the children came older lepers ghastly from fright. There was something pitiless and fear-inspiring in the brilliant moonlight that flooded the sky. As a rule, one associates the very idea of a hurricane with black darkness, or the lightning and the rain, but this tremendous gale across a clear sky leaped upon them like a visitation from another universe. It roused dense clouds of dust that without rising far above the earth, drove across the clearings into rolling, tumbling masses, glistening brown under the high moonlight. It whirled away the veranda from the Sisters' house, uprooted tall trees, and passed over the native cabins tearing them literally into shreds, and scattering the fragments out over the frantic, foaming Pacific.

The Sisters and a few of the men went out desperately into the vortex of the storm, dragging in bruised and stunned victims, to give them first aid. Mother Marianne encountered a blast that swept her off her feet, and carried her in air half across the clearing toward the sea, and possibly she owed her life to the clutch of a Hawaiian leper who caught at her in passing as he lay crouched on the ground. "Don't be afraid," he screamed through the howling tempest. "I am Imoku." He had been one of the lepers in the old Branch Hospital in Honolulu. His words came thin and far away across the colossal diapason of the gale. Father Wendelin was active in assisting, and Mother Marianne resumed her work, and continued the struggle from cottage to cottage to collect stragglers, and to drag them to spots of greater safety.

The Sisters' house shook and groaned, every timber crackled with its individual voice in protest under the maltreatment it received, and the apprehensive natives expected at every instant that this last haven would part from its moorings to mother earth, and reel away before the wind and into space, far out across the wild moon-silvered sea. Along the primeval skyline of the island, the feathery palms bent nearly double, flattened down before the storm, pointed wildly at the gray horizon; and the sea, whipped up at last into mountainous waves, rolled against the island cliffs with the thunderous shock of a long succession of great howitzer shells. The relation of the sea and the wind to the settlement will better be understood if it is recalled that the leper colony is on a peninsula projecting well out from the main body of the island.

This disturbance continued unabated till nearly ten o'clock, when a gray scud covered the sky, and in a few moments the rain began to fall in long horizontal sheets. But with the falling rain came a lessening in the gale, and its moaning voice abated, to be swallowed up in the ceaseless splash of falling waters. The receding hurricane had done its work.

Some distance down the road from the settlement the Mormons had a little church, and the lepers on venturing out at daybreak were astounded to see only bare ground where the building had been. Not a pane of glass nor a shingle, only bare earth in the green yard.

And the natives knew well, they said, that no other building could now be erected there, for clearly that spot was taboo. There was no shadow of doubt, to their way of thinking, that the spirits of the dead Chiefs had returned to the old haunts. The Sisters did all in their power to combat these superstitions, but their progress, as will be indicated later, was not altogether satisfactory. Old beliefs die hard.

Mother Marianne, following this visitation, began to make efforts to plant trees about the buildings, and about the whole plot. She sent abroad for seeds and shoots, and had friends procure good specimens, such as would grow well in this desolate earth and resist storm and drought obstinately. She tried hard

to import and acclimatize every shrub that seemed of
service, and little by little she made the Home look
better, but her work progressed slowly, both because
she had little help, and such jobs were attended to
only in the rare intervals between her multitudinous
official duties, and because from time to time her
neighbors appropriated property and carried it away
to be planted in their own yards. These thefts, coming from native and part-natives, could be overlooked to some extent; coming from whites and officials they were more serious.

IX

CAMILLA

MOTHER MARIANNE's troubles on Molokai were not confined to her struggle with dirt, disease, and typhoons. Amongst the resident lepers was no law, local or otherwise now, against marriage, and indeed many of the lepers had married after coming to Molokai. But many more had dispensed with the slender formalities custom presupposes, and numerous odd liaisons were the inevitable result. This situation was aggravated through the fantastic mixture of blood in the settlement, where nearly every variety of race, age, color, passion, and stage of disease had its representation. Medical people viewing the matter from a strictly scientific and sanitary point of view, were sceptical about these unions, though it had been well known for a long time that many babies born of leprous parents were themselves clean. But none of the authorities, medical or political, had found it possible, or perhaps had tried very hard, to check these irregular ways of living; possibly taking the view that as these hideous outcasts were doomed to death in any event, they might as well please themselves while they lived and saw the sun.

Mother Marianne, though in no position to legislate for people out of her domain, came quickly to the conclusion that if the Sisters' work on Molokai was to be a success, it would not only be advisable to keep the leprous women and girls apart for purposes of medical treatment, but in general to keep them segregated socially to prevent associations with a criminal element. Opium smoking seemed the most persistent habit, and the smugglers moved heaven and earth to get in their favorite goods; though to tell the truth, smugglers at Molokai had no different system from smugglers anywhere else on the seven seas. It appears that no final objections were raised to marriages in which there was some prospect of decent and reasonable support, and indeed some of the Sisters' patients married legally and were seemingly very happy for years. But Mother Marianne was especially anxious to prevent girls who were comparatively light cases from associating with male lepers far advanced, and vice versa, and strictly forbade her patients to leave the grounds without permission, or more particularly at night.

Naturally the news that a group of women and girls were living together, and in somewhat unprotected fashion, proved an immediate incentive to the more savage and lawless part of the settlement. A leprous girl called Camilla, who passed for a native but was uncommonly like a white girl in coloring and complexion, proved the focal point of trouble. She and a group of other lepers went bathing at a beach commonly avoided by the natives, who thought it possessed by "devil waves." Camilla came near drowning, and it was only with great difficulty that a native boatman rescued her. Apparently her charms moved him profoundly. Not very long after, he approached Mother Marianne with a request to adopt the girl. He was a far advanced case, and perhaps it was permissible to doubt that the adoption would have been all an adoption is supposed to be. At all events, taking her stand upon the obvious fact of his excessive disease, Mother Marianne refused.

He smiled as well as his face could smile, thanked her, and departed. Machiavelli could not have been more polite. In a few nights some native scouts appeared about the buildings, reconnoitering, apparently in preliminary preparation for a raid. Whites might have slept undisturbed through such stealthy leopard-like prowling, but the visitors were dealing also with native patients, as cautious, as cunning, and as wakeful as themselves. One of the sick girls woke to see a young man gliding through a window near her bed. He came across a band of bright moonlight with the speed and silence of a serpent, but the girl shrieked piercingly, and he turned to disappear into the outer darkness. She was unable to identify him.

Mother Marianne had a watch kept, but the invasions suddenly ceased, and night after night passed peacefully, with only the ocean wind blowing in the trees, and the long roll of the Pacific splashing in low thunder on the shore. The watchers saw, or professed to see, nothing. Mother Marianne waited, in deep concern.

Then, one night, some weeks later, as she made her rounds, she found Camilla was not in her ward. A search was begun at once. There were wide green fields around that offered little cover, the moon glowing like a vast fiery pearl flooded them with tropic brilliance. The Sisters and their helpers hunted over the ground from the Home to the Damien Road, and when almost ready to give up the search, saw at last at a little carriage house, far back from the road, several figures emerging. In a few moments Camilla and another girl, not previously missed, came back to the Home.

Mother Marianne asked where they had been.

Camilla was brief and to the point. "We were with some men."

"I am afraid," said Mother Marianne, "that I cannot allow you to remain in the Home."

Camilla and her friend, apparently well satisfied, packed their scanty baggage and left.

Shortly after this adventurous pair departed, two Chinese lepers, an old woman, Ah Lin, and her daughter, Ah Kyan, filled their places. The girl was beautiful, well and strongly built, with a good complexion, brilliant eyes, and an attractive ease and grace in all her movements; a very charming child and such a light case that no one would believe her leprous. Her mother was in a bad way, and everyone expected the old woman to die in a little while.

Within a few days after this fascinating girl had entered the Home she drew the attention of a young Americanized Chinese who lived near and made money by distilling liquors, and conducting a small gambling house where lepers could shoot craps, or play at blackjack or stud. His methods of earning money were either unknown to, or ignored by, the civil authorities, and as some of the condemned men were wealthy in their own rights and others had relatives who pitied them and furnished them freely with all they asked for, some very flourishing games occurred in the Chinese shack.

Ah Kyan was the devoted slave of her mother, thinking no effort too great if it tended to the old lady's comfort. Mother Marianne naturally admired this filial devotion, and Ah Kyan in turn did what she could to please the superior, whom she seemed honestly to like.

When the young Chinese gambler came to the Home, and asked for Ah Kyan, a match was arranged with less than the usual difficulty. Ah Kyan had already seen and admired him, her mother wanted to get her married, the man was wealthy, personable and kind and, like Ah Kyan, a very light case. Mother Marianne, after surveying the situation, arrived at the conclusion that marriage would be a good-enough solution, the more so as the principals seemed to want each other very much. And to do her critical acumen justice, she had not misjudged the man. He made Ah Kyan a good husband.

The young people took Ah Lin to live with them, and did all they could to make her days pleasant. Both Ah Lin and Ah Kyan were baptized, and became Catholics. Ah Kyan was a shrewd girl who would have gone far, given better circumstances. The husband remained non-committal, but promised to ponder seriously upon the matter of religion.

From time to time Ah Kyan came back to the Home to visit with the girls, but suddenly her trips became irregular and short, and she was obviously worried. One day, after a considerable absence had intervened, she came and without going near the sick took Sister Leopoldina's arm and led her aside. She said, "I did not come here to see the girls. I came to tell you something, and then I must go back quickly.

"Some days ago a party came to play cards with my husband. A native, Nakipi, Camilla's husband, was the leader."

"So Camilla is still living?" Sister Leopoldina asked.

"Yes, but she is failing, and wasting away. I think poor Camilla will soon die. He treats her so badly. When Nakipi and his crowd come to my house, my husband told me I should go and spend my evenings with my friends. And that it was not good for me to be at home when that crowd was there. Something in my head told me they were no good, and I thought I must know why they dislike me—and hear what they talk about.

"So I put a big black cloak on my head, and I creep close to the house till I come under the open window where they play cards and drink rum. And I can hear all the talk. Nakipi leads the other boys. They plan bad things for Mother Marianne. They say they must get rid of her. A long time I stay there, and I hear them talk.

"And now I am sad, for if they do harm to Mother Marianne, my husband has trouble, and oh, Sister, he is good to my mother and me. And I was mad at the men. I rush into the house, and when they see me, they all sit very still. Then they go away. But they come again, afterward, and my husband always tells me to go away, and I always go under the window and listen.

"Then I come to the Home and tell the girls everything. I hear Nakipi say, 'At twelve o'clock next night the moon is dark, we go. It is a good time. We not meet here, but one by one go to the Home, and hide in the barn. At twelve we knock on the door, and when she opens, we gag her so she cannot scream, and carry her off before anyone can tell who we are.'"

The Sister listening to this began to feel a sensation as if the solid ground under her feet were heaving and dissolving. She said, "It is tonight?"

"Tonight at twelve. But all the native women here know about it, and they are going to help Mother Marianne."

"How can I thank you?"

"I do not want thanks. I love Mother. I am ashamed my husband should have these men in my house."

She turned and walked out.

The Sister inquired amongst the native women and found that Ah Kyan's tale was true. They knew, and were very excited. They had taken matters into their own hands. All the light cases were assembled. One huge native remarked grimly, "It will be a battle!"

It was not so many generations since the days when the big island women fought beside their men, with bludgeons and spears, in the old wars, and now their descendants were sharpening butcher knives and cutting clubs, in stealthy preparation for another civil feud quite as furious as any that had preceded. The natives were muscular as tigresses, and could be just as blindly ferocious, as Melville noticed long before in "Typee."

There was a fence around the front yard, and the Amazons came to the conclusion that their best plan of attack was to encircle the house, coming up from the rear in two parties, so that when the abductors were on the front porch they could be taken from both sides and at the back. The ringing of a dinner bell would give the alarm. Mother Marianne was not informed.

The Sister got a shudder when she came upon Kahiana, a tall, sinewy, brown girl, sitting on the floor and with great expenditure of perspiration and effort, sharpening a hatchet on a brick. The Sister noticed with discomfort that the blade shone like silver. "Why, Kahiana, what are you going to do?"

"I'm going to kill them dirty men if they come."

To lovers of melodrama it is disconcerting that no battle transpired. For when the kidnappers arrived and noticed some of the preparations that could not be concealed, they understood everything, and after waiting and talking matters over for a while, finally withdrew almost as stealthily as they had arrived.

It was significant of the violent, nervous effects such excitement exerted amongst these lepers that Nakipi died in a little while after, and Ah Kyan also from a light case became suddenly severe, wasted, and with other complications, in a few weeks passed away. The husband brought Ah Lin back to the Home. She who had been expected to die months and months before, still lived on like the Ancient Mariner, while all around her fell and expired. With her came, too, the young Camilla, now a walking skeleton, creeping back to the Home to end the brief remnant of her days.

At their passing, the Chinese gambler, who seems to have loved Ah Kyan with a strange and surpassing devotion, closed up his books, ceased his pursuits which held no further interest and prepared also for death, which visited him shortly. But big, bushy-haired Kahiana, with her silver bright hatchet, survived for many a year, and watched over Mother

Marianne with a fidelity rarely rivaled, and was always a helper at the Home.

Among such troubles Mother Marianne lived daily.

X

EXPERIENCES

Following Father Damien's death, many troubles developed amongst his leper associates. He had never, of course, been able to make friends with all the men whom he wished to have in his parish. Many had avoided him, others who lived on the mountain sides were wild as panthers, and shunned equally all religious and civilized influences, and finally there was the usual complement of backsliders who infest every community.

To endeavor to collect the fragments of this scattered group, and to give them something of a mother's care, was a herculean task, as Mr. Dutton and Mother Marianne soon found. But the Sister had given Father Damien a promise that she would try to take care of the motherless children at his parish, and try she did. The trip from Bishop Home, however, was a long and exhausting affair.

Therefore, a Portuguese called Manuel and his wife who lived near the Home, were induced to help, and the Board of Health furnished a horse and carriage. The horse was wild, and though Manuel boasted that the horse he could not control did not live, it was clear that every time he took Mother Marianne to the Damien settlement she went with her life in her hands.

The horse would run away; little, fiery, waspish, dark Manuel would saw wildly and unsuccessfully at the bit, and the carriage would bound like a mad thing over roads that owed their designation only to politeness, and more nearly resembled the shell-torn sides of that famous hill at Verdun, Le Mort Homme. Manuel's blazing temper and equally blazing vocabulary, and the rashness with which he courted disaster by whipping the mare when, at the outset, she needed no excuse to run like a maniac, all alarmed and distressed Mother Marianne. Every trip to the Damien parish was a nightmare to her and her companion, Sister Vincent, and they were shaken and jolted nearly into nervous prostration. Despite Mother Marianne's objections, Manuel decided after a month, to teach this mare a lesson. She was a high-spirited beast, and he committed the indignity of hitching her to a dump cart. Then he took the lines, braced his feet, and laid on the lash. Presumably she was already meditating reprisals, for she gave a leap that nearly unseated him, and started, not down the road, but straight across country, at a rate that made Tam O'Shanter's ride seem mild. The Sisters watched in tearful panic while the awkward cart executed one mad gyration after another, plunging down into deep ruts and holes and rearing up over boulders, till it disappeared into a cloud of dust.

A somewhat chastened Manuel returned much later, leading the mare which had a few remnants of harness still dangling from her. Mother Marianne did not know whether to be angry or to laugh. The cart was almost a total wreck, and it was only by the utmost exertions that pieces could be retrieved which could be repaired into a semblance of the original vehicle. The horse was so battered and bleeding from collision with rocks and brambles and tree trunks that Mother Marianne thought it would be necessary to shoot her. Manuel nursed her through, however, and the two equally high-spirited and unreasonable creatures finally became fast friends.

Amid such scenes Mother Marianne pushed on her work amongst the sick in the Damien parish, washing and dressing their sores, preparing, and administering their medicines according to the doctors' prescriptions, and recording the reactions for the benefit of the medical folk who worked with them, making their beds for and bathing the helpless ones, and in the intervals recommending to them a somewhat more Christian way of living than seemed to suit many.

Yet she was singularly successful, due mainly to force of character and example; for the sick had early learned the difference between Mother Marianne and many helpers of another ilk who came to them. She was deeply sincere and what she told them she believed. One good deed has more weight than a shelf full of sermons, and her preaching, like that of Peter Claver, was of the penetrating variety which deals in facts rather than in theories. Under these circumstances the mission throve in spite of her troubles; her charges came to love her with that strange and ultimate affection that binds people together in time and eternity, and knowing she would be parted from them only by death, they strove hard to please her. There was no cant or self-seeking here.

Nor did she ever lose sight of the labors of her helpers in other islands. In a letter dated August 18, 1892, she writes:

"I was absent from the leper settlement from July 3rd to the 28th. I spent 10 days in Wailuku at the request of Sister Bonaventure. Sister Ludovica and Sister Antonia are not very well but both are at their posts. Sister Antonia has a large school—80 girls—which is a hard task for her. . . . During my absence Sister Leopoldina and Sister Elizabeth were alone here—you may be sure I received a warm welcome on my return home."

And the *home* she returns to is a leper settlement!

Mother Marianne put Sister Crescentia in charge of the work among leper boys, and sent Sisters Vincent and Renata to assist her. Mr. Dutton did much of the heavier labor with the sick. This good man was invaluable in the little crises that continually arose amongst some of the more child-like natives, for he, too, exerted that spiritual and intellectual authority that arises from sheer honesty of purpose, sincerity of belief, and kindness in execution. The preparation for and the construction of new buildings was not without its difficulties, and some quarrelings among the jealous and suspicious ones. As the outcome of part of this trouble, the superintendent of the leper settlement, a Mr. Evans, was seized and roughly handled by the lepers, who also threatened to kill Father Conrardy but lacked courage to go through with their plans.

Evans went away to Honolulu after this fraças, and a police force had finally to be sent out to Molokai. Mother Marianne then asked Mr. Dutton to take over such duties as the superintendent had had. He was glad to comply, and his experience made him invaluable. Following the death of Father Damien, the Sisters had charge of and were active in the work amongst leper men and boys for six years. Then, at Mother Marianne's request, the Board of Health obtained Father Damien's own brother, an old professor, with four brothers of the Sacred Hearts of Jesus and Mary, who came from Europe to continue the work, and particularly to take care of the new Baldwin Home for men and boys at Kalawao. As this was something of a relief to the Sisters, who had need for all their forces at the Bishop Home, they now withdrew. The Baldwin Home, built chiefly with money contributed by the generous Henry P. Baldwin of Maui, was opened and occupied in May, 1894. It is on a good location, and owes much of its attractive surroundings to the tireless labor of Mr. Dutton, who planted over five thousand eucalyptus trees, landscaped the grounds, cleared away rubbish and stones and generally made the site possible and practicable.

By way of passing comment upon these disorders amongst the natives and the troubles so many white men had with them, one finds a very significant remark in Sister Leopoldina's diary; to the effect that the pure bred native men had such high regard for the Sisters and in general for all white women who deserved it, that though sharp differences of opinion did occur, no Hawaiian man had ever insulted one of the Sisters or had been openly disrespectful; and this entry in spite of the fact that desperate half-castes had on two occasions fomented plots to kidnap or kill Mother Marianne. As a rule, however, the part-natives showed poorer qualities than the true natives.

While these matters were going on in Molokai, the old Kapiolani Home at Honolulu was left as it was, even when the Receiving Station was broken up. It was the wish of many members of the Legislature to break up the Home also, and the president of the Board of Health requested Father Leonor to send the children then in the Kapiolani Home to some boarding school (ignoring the fact that boarding schools did not want and would not receive them); offering to have the Board of Health pay their expenses. It is entirely beside the purpose of this narrative to discuss island politics; but it is lamentably evident that much of the activity of certain departments that should be strictly non-partisan, for example, the public health service, was riddled by crafty political schemers. In a word, island politics were about as unscrupulous, treacherous and low as politics in our own country.

It was owing to the efforts of Mother Marianne, her expressed wish and her devoted labor, that the Kapiolani Home was retained for the time. Ultimately, after many changes in Honolulu affairs, the Kapiolani girls were moved to a new building with an adjacent convent for the Sisters, and the nuns with them again took charge of work among the lepers.

Experiences

New Sisters came from the States, and some were assigned shortly to Molokai. Another shift occurred when a plague broke out in Honolulu, and the Sisters and their wards were taken to a detention camp; an unpleasant place far down the beach, where hundreds of wild ducks and other waterfowl splashed and screamed on the shallow mud flats all day long under the broiling sun, and though the plague presently abated, here the children remained, and all the work had to be carried on, for twelve long years, before the United States government stepped in and built their present beautiful home on the mountainside.

To return to Molokai, and Mother Marianne's work amongst the natives, the girls at the Bishop Home and the boys at the Baldwin Home. The old native superstitions were not dead, and from time to time, in places back from the coast, the lepers gathered to celebrate ancient rites, and at intervals dim stories about their practices reached the settlement. None of the more responsible whites were initiated, and as the natives, even the better class, kept particularly to themselves these fantastic affairs in honor of the old gods, it was difficult for the workers at the hospital or at either of the Homes to get an exact inkling of what the people did and believed.

But one night, for example, when some boys went up on the mountain and fastened lanterns to kites, the sick girls in the hospital saw the blazing flames in air and began to scream. Questioned, they admitted they thought the fire in view was the evil flying prayer of a magician who was praying someone to death. There was something fantastic and horrible in the idea, as readers of Rossetti's "Sister Helen" will recall.

It gave the white folk an eerie feeling to realize that in the shadows of the mountain gorges, in the deep forests, on the lonely peaks, strange and destructive forces assembled to renew ancient rites. It was as if one were walking amid unseen things which stood aside and gibbered soundlessly as he went by, but would not desert his path. So many of the native superstitions had their roots deep in the past and were founded upon practices and beliefs of centuries gone, that combating them was like asking the islander to change his very nature. Yet, with a certain calm assurance, the Sisters did this very thing, and in spite of their pagan surroundings came to no harm because of all these mysterious events.

Some true understanding of their situation was necessary if the newcomers were to get along with their savage charges. For instance, because a tribe has judged it imperative in the past to sacrifice a human being to secure regular rainfall, is no reason for continuing the custom; but for the civilized man to begin his acquaintance with the savage by ridiculing what the savage regarded as sacred and serious, is far from the best way to get on with him. Men rise out of barbarism only by almost imperceptible degrees, and sometimes lapse back into it very suddenly. Understanding, above all else, a penetrating intelligence, and the readiness to meet another's viewpoint, as far as is possible, are the requisites for any diplomat who would preach a true gospel. Mother Marianne possessed these qualities in the highest degree.

Under her régime there was no trouble with the charges because of these sporadic revivals of ancient pagan religion. Nor did serious trouble arise even when patients discovered that the hospital was peopled by ghosts. "This house is full of ghosts," said a girl dying of leprosy.

"Did you see them?" asked a Sister.

"No. But I heard them walking around, and eating, and they were making such a noise I could not sleep all night. I was so much afraid." And, again, a day or two later, "It was frightful. Such a strange noise, and a heavy walking through the house. I cannot sleep. It is going on the whole night!"

In this sick and unhealthy atmosphere, ghosts thus became a continual nuisance. Some of the natives saw ghosts regularly and frequently, while others could hear only a heavy trampling about the building at night, presumably, they said, the heavy footfalls of the old Hawaiian chiefs returned to persecute those who had abandoned the ancient practices of worship. Some of the cottages seemed particularly affected, and the Sisters found it difficult in the extreme to get the sick folk out of this unhappy frame of mind.

Hallucinations? Possibly. Science explains so many things, but not the human mind. That still possesses unfathomable mysteries. But the sick girl, who was gently encouraged to have confidence in her friends, to disregard the imagined visitations of shadowy ancient chiefs, and to have recourse to certain practical prayers and meditations when she felt disturbed, finally found the whole matter gradually clarified. Thus, with a new viewpoint substituted for a former state of indecision, the child-like mind was led to be at rest. The ghosts ceased to trample and crash in the echoing rooms.

To poets of a tragic turn, one might say that if there were ghosts, surely Molokai would be the place for them. There, so many people have suffered horribly and died, that their very agony seems to have permeated the grim landscape, and the island has become a gaunt monument to their woe. In some sensitive souls it evokes a shudder to walk across certain battlefields in northern France, for since Julius Cæsar, literally millions of men have soaked this ground with their life blood. Battles innumerable, savage, stupid, interminable, have torn its soil. If there are ghosts, they dwell on these old battlefields. If there are ghosts, they should be on Molokai, too.

But fortunately, Mother Marianne and her helpers were religious and sincere people who had work to do, the work of easing pain and banishing fear, and they did it with consummate skill that springs only from love of humanity and love of God. When the work at the Baldwin Home was well under way, and the boys were being better attended to, Mr. Bishop besides donating the money for the Home that bears his name, gave a considerable sum for the building of a chapel and other conveniences for the Sisters. It is not large, but it is high and white, and between it and the convent is a room into which lepers can come, so that they may hear the celebration of the Mass. Prior to this construction, the lepers had experienced difficulty in performing their religious duties, for lepers were not allowed to go into the convent itself. Even Father Damien stayed outside. Mr. Bishop's generosity has made a lasting and deep impression. A number of other improvements were effected;

specially to secure warm water for bathing the sick, as this had always been a problem in the past, and heating water slowly over a stove the only method.

One summer morning, a year after Father Damien's death, the ocean was mild and a quiet breeze rustled the trees. A blazing splendor of golden clouds surrounded the sun, forecasting another hot day. The settlement lay quietly in that baking sunshine in a somnolent silence when a steamer glided around in the shade of the great mountain, and lowered a boat. The party that came ashore contained King Kalakaua.

At noon Mother Marianne assembled the Sisters for a formal meeting, and the sovereign accompanied by several English officers came to the convent parlor. Greetings exchanged, he drew his chair closer to Mother Marianne, and said directly, "Madame, we have spent the whole morning going about the settlement trying to find a proper place to erect Father Damien's monument. And we have failed to find a suitable spot. So we have come to have you tell us where to place it."

In a gracious way peculiarly her own she replied "I have often thought a nice place for it would be at the foot of the hill, just outside the home grounds, by the side of the Damien Road, where people passing on the road can see it, and it can easily be seen by people on the steamers."

"Madame, kindly come and show us the place, and it shall be put there."

The King rose and stepped aside to let her pass, and Mother Marianne led them to the spot. She pointed out the exact site she preferred, and Kalakaua offering his hand, said, "This is a proper place. It shall be as you wish."

The party left as quietly and unostentatiously as it had come.

XI

THE TURN OF THE CENTURY

MOTHER MARIANNE had apparently never been quite well, and the hard work she did here made matters steadily worse. In spite of the fact that the government was spending much money upon the leper settlement, and a great deal of the heavy work was supposed to be taken care of, there remained a vast amount of rough and ready pioneering. Mother Marianne and some of the more active girls even gathered stones and broken rock to fill in deep cuts in the construction of a walk across the fields, working day after day at this laborious task till their hands were chipped and bleeding, and they were completely exhausted. Of course, some of her friends expostulated, using the old, well-tried, and quite truthful arguments, that she ought not to wear herself out in such menial tasks, but should wait till the government or some charitably inclined philanthropist would get it done for her. For any worker who was determined to be very conserving of her own energy, these representations would have had sufficient weight, for indeed their reasonableness was clear enough. But to this brilliant and devoted mind who had not come out to Molokai to spare herself, but to work, and who considered herself "expendable" as military folk say, and who believed that destroyed she could be readily replaced, as a soldier killed in action is replaced by another just as good, there was but one answer, to grapple with all the work that presented itself. Besides, when one waits for dilatory officialdom to get something done, one is likely to be waiting a long time, and if Mother Marianne had depended upon politicians and the Board for the completion of some of these tasks, many of them would not be completed to this day.

King Kalakaua died January 20, 1891, and his wife Kapiuolani left the palace never to return. His sister Liliuokalani replaced him, a large woman, coarse featured and very dark. She had married an Englishman, and spoke English fluently. She came out to Molokai, after a time, upon a tour of inspection. Few things bespeak more eloquently the rulers' nervous dread of leprosy than the concern felt amongst otherwise unfeeling politicians over the battle being waged against this still mysterious disease.

Mother Marianne welcomed the party, and the

lepers in native fashion greeted their new ruler with a program of songs. Liliuokalani was not affected. She wore a plain black holoku, without ornament of any kind, and the native red and yellow wreath around her neck. It was noticeable that she spoke no word of welcome or of thanks when the lepers had completed their parts, and they retired from the royal presence much abashed at her cool reaction to their efforts. In a few minutes her medical staff returned from their visit to the lepers' cottages, and the whole party left, the Queen still in the same cold hard silence. She created a distinctly unfavorable impression amongst her subjects on Molokai.

Some of the royal party were suffering from *la grippe,* and on departing they seemed to have left it behind, for Mother Marianne soon found it raging everywhere, and her supply of quinine and other medicines was nearly wiped out in combating it.

From time to time there occurred curious tragedies related to leprosy though not of it. One girl, a little Hawaiian called Ella, spent years on Molokai. She seemed quite clean, but she had remarkable swellings just under the skin on her hands, her wrists, and her forearms. These looked for all the world like the familiar lumps that gathered on the true lepers' joints. It did not come out until years afterward that shortly before she had first been suspected of leprosy and examined, she had been dreadfully beaten by a teacher in one of the grade schools of Honolulu. For some minor fault, this worthy had used a heavy cane on the child till the bones of the hands and wrists were bruised and chipped, and the huge swellings that resulted never entirely abated. By the time the doctors were finally, unwillingly, convinced she was not leprous, she had nearly grown up, and having gotten along well at the Home where they were all quite fond of her, she gave up all thought of ever leaving, convinced herself that somehow she was a leper, and felt resigned to stay. Indeed she was by now (eleven years had passed in her exile) well enough satisfied to remain.

The doctor in charge, Oliver, then secured permission from the Board of Health for another examination and review of her case, and Ella was officially pronounced no leper. So, about the time she was finally well settled, and had struck root so to speak, bureaucracy ordered the roots torn up, and Ella returned to Honolulu. But, as one can readily understand, she never since lost a deep and bitter resentment for the mingled stupidity and cruelty that had cost her eleven years of her life. It seems as strange as if one had seen them in a dream, to observe these extraordinary cases, sometimes pathetic or grotesque, sometimes humorous or ironic, passing through the kaleidoscope of life on Molokai. They are like queer impossible figments of a diseased imagination, caught in some strange mold, and held fixed forever, creatures of an opium eater's fancy, not related to real life, yet, tragically, just in the center of it.

To preserve one's equanimity in the midst of such blundering and futility was a task for the ablest of diplomats. One wonders how a sensitive and refined woman did not go mad on this prison island. But Mother Marianne continued steadily at her post, and exerted as days went on a remarkably increasing influence for good upon all who came under her care.

She wrote most of her reports, letters, and other papers at night, between ten o'clock and one o'clock in the morning, when the settlement was usually quiet. Her incessant work by day left her indeed very little other time for writing. The documents are very interesting, written in a beautiful even flowing script that betokens perfect ease and control in the composer; a tribute to her power of mind that when her aching weary muscles were worn down by the day's exertions she could still secure a balance and dignity and ease from the power of her will.

The necessity that weighed upon her for keeping the lepers employed, and indeed the advantages of employment from the purely psychological standpoint, drove her to many expedients, but few efforts were put to better use than lace making. She taught all the girls who were interested enough to learn, and whose hands would permit them to work. The progress of the disease had indeed disabled the fingers of some to an extent that rendered fine handiwork an impossibility. The girls made lace, and one called Luka sold it among folk adjacent to the Sister's part of the settlement. Not only did the girls learn to make good lace, but they kept their minds occupied at their simple tasks, forgot for a time what leprosy means, and finally when Luka took their finished product out to sell, realized a small but welcome profit from their exertions.

Meanwhile, at about ten minutes' walk from the yard, a cottage was constructed to which some of the lepers could be taken when it was desirable to have them away from the hospital for a little time. There was an enormous tree with waxy dark leaves which threw a broad shade over the surrounding plain, and did not seem ever to feel the heat of summer, or the drought. The sick children had liked to play around this tree, and here the cottage was built; the lepers called it their Ever Green Home. A driveway was constructed from the Home to the great tree, and on both sides, all the way up, Mother Marianne and her charges dug deep holes and planted date palms. The digging, planting, and watering, were an untold amount of work, but it kept the lepers occupied and pleased, and in the end well repaid the efforts.

As these planting and growing days went on, Mother Marianne occasionally had opportunity for amusement of the more cynical kind. One of the various superintendents who controlled governmental activities on Molokai once came to Bishop Home, and blandly told the good Sister, "I want to beautify my residence. There will be a reward given by some members of the Legislature for the most beautifully kept home grounds. They will be here as usual in April."

He wanted the best of Mother Marianne's plants and flowers. She was astounded by this effrontery, but finally said he could have some. He sent some men, with a number of carts, and without so much as "By your leave" they dug up the finest shrubs and small trees, together with a few of the larger trees as well, and hauled them away leaving the gardens at Bishop Home looking much as though a typhoon had passed through. He remarked candidly, "I'll turn my place into a paradise. They will be surprised, and wonder how I could get them to grow big so quickly!"

As Mother Marianne had devoted a great deal of

time and effort to planting fine flowers and to obtaining good plants both in the islands and abroad, while her friends in the tropics and elsewhere, had at considerable expense gathered many bushes for her, she had, naturally, some splendid specimens. That they were private property seemed to make little difference to this piece of officialdom.

Unhappily his native envoys forgot some alligator pear trees. Mother Marianne was not sorry, as she had a special liking for the victims thus overlooked. But the gentleman telephoned that evening. His voice was sharp and bold. He said to Sister Leopoldina who answered the 'phone. "Sister, you tell Mother I want her alligator pear trees. She didn't send them!"

"How many do you want?"

"I want all of them."

Mother Marianne had refused to quarrel over the matter, perhaps regarding the source of the insult as unworthy of an altercation, but Sister Leopoldina justly lost her temper. "You will not have one of them," she said, and banged down the receiver with a force that made his ear crack.

She expected a rebuke from her superior, and turned around ready to take it, but saw Mother Marianne, her features contorted with suppressed laughter, and with her hands half over her face.

"Sister," she said, "how could you have done that?"

"He needed someone to bring him to his senses," said the sturdy Leopoldina.

Mother Marianne and the superintendent came shortly to a more serious clash when he decided to tear down the wall around the Bishop Home grounds, and to put some pig sties up the wind from the hospital. Mother Marianne's determined opposition finally caused the abandonment of the scheme. But some time later her date palms were torn up and carted away by night. To no avail, of course, as date palms hardly ever stand transplanting when well grown.

She remained as calm and serene before petty thieving officials as before the more vigorous desperadoes who had threatened her life. Political activities lay apart from the work in the leper settlement, but nevertheless it was with a feeling of great satisfaction that the staff saw the Stars and Stripes raised over the Hawaiian Islands on September 11, 1898. Union with the United States meant more freedom, probably better governmental aid, and some more systematic medical efforts to destroy leprosy. The native government had indeed meant well, and had worked hard, though sometimes irregularly against the scourge.

The Turn of the Century

An excellent new church was built, and on June 27, 1900, the Bishop of Honolulu arrived. On June 29, formally, the new church was blessed by the Bishop. There was a long procession, and many societies attended.

The care extended to the children is well illustrated in a letter Mother Marianne wrote to Dr. C. B. Cooper, president of the Board of Health, Honolulu, August 14, 1903.

"During these years it has been customary to take the children to the valleys Waikolu, Waileia and Waihauau. Often we have taken them out three and four times a week for guavas or mountain apples during the fruit season; to the sea to get sea-moss for their table, to gather shells for fancy work; and to bathe in the sea when they desired to do so. We do not allow them to go to the Chinese coffee shops, or to roam about the settlement at will."

Mother Marianne had not been very well for years, although she never complained, and indeed her companions were only occasionally aware of her trouble. But on one occasion when a group of girls had wanted to walk to the Waikolu valley, some nine miles away, and a companion was needed, Mother Marianne had gone with them, and as the day developed a terrific and unusual heat, all the party came home exhausted, and feeling nearly sick. She had not been well since then, but her weakness latterly increased, and culminated in two violent hemorrhages which left her very weak and helpless. She had suffered repeatedly from pulmonary hemorrhages which would seem to indicate tuberculosis, but if she had this disease it must have remained somewhat stationary, and her last illness was a dropsy. Doctor Oliver, then in Honolulu on a brief vacation, was summoned back to the island, and did what he could. He prescribed a complete rest, and after some two months, she was apparently able to take her work as usual. At all events, except for an increasing pallor and lassitude, she seemed to be very much as before, and her cheerful conversation and manner rather deceived her companions who thought the recovery extraordinarily complete and rapid.

When she resumed her duties there was much to be done. The usual social troubles continued. Indeed they never entirely ceased. One night at eleven o'clock there was a sharp rap at the front door. When Mother Marianne opened it, she discovered a remarkably beautiful Hawaiian girl whom she had never seen before. "What do you want?" asked the superior.

"My husband."

Mother Marianne's amazement could better be imagined than described. "Your husband is not here. I don't know you."

"Yes, he is here. He is in Hana's room." She talked a few moments, and added details.

Hana was one of the best trusted of the inmates.

Mother Marianne went with Sister Leopoldina to the cabin in question and knocked. Hana came to the door in her nightdress, and rubbing her eyes. The room behind her was dark.

"Are you alone?" asked Mother Marianne.

"Yes, I'm alone."

Mother Marianne said sharply, speaking past her and calling the man by name, "Kaliohana! Come out here."

He came, somewhat sheepishly, crawling from under the bed.

"Go. I never want to see your face again," said the superior.

He went, but before morning Hana had packed her bags and left, too. Death claimed husband, and wife, and Hana, within a few months.

In a letter written on November 5, 1903, Mother Marianne remarks:

"On next Sunday it will be twenty years since we arrived in Honolulu—just think, twenty years—. On the 14th it will be 15 years since we came to the leper island—. How the time slips away from us—How many more years will it please God to permit us to work for Him? is a question ever before me. I am not well, neither am I sick—but

I am growing old and am not able to do as much work as I wish to do—we have to pull hard to keep this cart going.

"Please pray for us that God may keep us in the future as He has so mercifully done in the years we have spent here among the unclean. Just now we have 98 women and girls in the Home; some very bad cases. Ten are totally blind, ten are able to see a little and will soon lose the little sight they have."

Other troubles followed, and pressed hard upon the nursing staff. On one occasion the Hawaiian lepers at Molokai came near to starvation, and in a peculiar manner, as they still had food obtainable. The black plague ravaged the island, and so great was the dread it caused that most of the captains of small freighters refused to stop at the island, to approach the wharf, or indeed to bring in any food. Most of the Hawaiians depended chiefly upon their native *poi* for subsistence, and when the supply failed (for their friends elsewhere who usually sent them things were now unable to get in touch with them) they felt that they were, literally, starving. The Sisters endeavored to get them to substitute rice, and this went well enough with the Chinese and Japanese cases, but to the natives nothing could replace their *poi*, and many of them became seriously sick and others suffered as much as if they were actually starving.

American workers inexperienced among the islanders found this situation difficult to understand, but
older heads who knew the natives well were very
much depressed, and made unavailing efforts to procure *poi*. The sickness that followed was sporadic,
but apparently severe, and the victims suffered a
great deal. It is often said by people unfamiliar with
leprosy and the innumerable hideous complications
that it drags in its train that lepers do not suffer
much. It is true that some cases do sometimes fall
into a lethargy, but keen agony is also common and
frequent to numbers. The pangs of semi-starvation
made their case the more pitiable.

Years went by and many changes occurred. The
sick died, and more sick took their places. The endless procession of misery went on. A new superintendent, an excellent man called McVeigh, came, and
exerted himself vigorously for the sufferers. An
American doctor, Goodhue, arrived, a good surgeon
and a very energetic man. He made great improvements.

The government report of June 30, 1904 (page
65), *in re* Bishop Home, reads "The good Mother
[Marianne] and Sisters have more work than they
can, or should be asked to, perform. They have
labored among our leper charges for over twenty
years without complaining of the increasing work,

without vacation or rest, and from my own personal observation of their daily work [the superintendent J. D. McVeigh is writing], the breaking down point is not very far off. I would suggest that the Board seek to persuade two more Sisters to come here and assist in this noble work."

Occasionally government reports make better reading when interpreted with the aid of a little comment. A few glosses, or scholia, as the scholar would say. Here follows a quotation from page seven of the report of the president of the Board of Health for the six months ending June 30, 1905. *In re* Kapiolani Home in Honolulu for non-leprous female children of lepers:

"It was my privilege to conduct a committee of the recent Legislature on a visit to the above-named institution. It was certainly a revelation and almost a rebuke, when they observed the improvements made solely by the labor of the regular employees and girl inmates of the Home under the supervision of the good Sisters. From old materials given them they have erected a large dormitory and accessories. An additional appropriation of $500.00 afterwards greatly assisted toward proper plumbing and sanitary arrangements.

"The committee were visibly affected and were in the mood to consider, and then and there promised to provide for the needs of the non-leprous boys—children of lepers—which subject was urgently brought to their attention.

"The Kapiolani Home is now very comfortable, and all the inmates are apparently contented, healthy, and happy."

What the good man did not say, and perhaps did not know, was that Sister Benedicta who was in charge got very tired of being put off with empty promises when she asked for better accommodations for the children in her care. So she went ahead and built with the help of the yard men. She never was one to let obstacles stand in her way. She was being put off on her requests because some local politicians wanted the Home closed. So she got permission to use some old discarded lumber from another building, and the officials never dreamed she would build a large dormitory with it!

But it is more likely that the president had an inkling of the truth. His above-quoted remark "a revelation and almost a rebuke" seems too significant to be coincidence.

The same report shows that on June 30, 1905, there were 907 lepers in the colony on Molokai.

That the Kapiolani Home was really in hard straits is indicated in a similar report (page 30) for the six months ending December 31, 1906. "The

Sisters of St. Francis have here done a remarkable work. They have been sadly neglected. Matters have come to a desperate pass. There are 45 girls with 9 other persons, or 54 in all, to be supported on $319.17 per month, or $6.09 each per month, except the small salaries paid (to lay helpers), and this pitiful amount has to supply food, clothing, schooling, improvements, repairs, maintenance, etc. This can no longer be done on so small a sum."

Many years were clocked off since the Sisters had come to Molokai, and in most of that time they had had only the most inadequate aid and resources; for example, one nursing Sister to do all the dressing.

On June 2, 1908, Mother Marianne states clearly the case of the work in Hawaii, in a letter to Reverend Mother Johanna.

". . . you are aware that we out here are all growing old, and consequently are not able to go on with the heavy work we have been doing in the past. In Honolulu at the Kapiolani Home are three Sisters; all three worn out and more than half sick. They have fifty-six children to care for, many of them mere infants who require care night and day. Every week the letters from there tell me of their hardships and the need of help. I am helpless. Is there any hope for more help in the near future? Here at Molokai we are five Sisters, and have our hands full. I am over seventy years old. You can judge from that."

XII

AN EASTER FEAST

It may be of interest to know how the islanders enjoyed an average Easter. One Saturday morning before Easter Sunday it was dark and cloudy. The air was cool and men could work rapidly without becoming exhausted. Two men who were non-lepers dug a great hole in the ground, and filled it with layers of kindling and good hard wood. Over the top of the wood, when it was leveled off, they laid a layer of fairly broad stones. Through a little opening that was left, they started a fire at the bottom. And while this tremendous concentrated conflagration was surging up and was heating the stones, they killed a very large fat hog. After cleaning it, they cut it in one hundred and ten pieces.

About twenty women and girls joined the party, sitting in two rows on the grass in the shade of the *poi* house, and facing each other, and it was fascinating to an onlooker to see their fingers fly as they tied up each piece of pork, attaching a slice of salt salmon to it to season it. Each of these little bundles was wrapped up in long green ti leaves. And all the time, the roaring glaring flames were heating the stones to a lava-like glow.

When at last the wood had become a deep bed of scarlet coals, covered with stones almost equally scarlet, and smoke had ceased to curl up, a thick layer of wide green banana leaves was flung over the stones, and on them were laid the hundred and ten bundles of pork and salmon; all around the pork, nicely disposed in rows lay more than a hundred of the best large sweet potatoes available.

On top of all this they heaped more ti and banana leaves. And, again, over this layer they laid rows of rice and sugar bags. And, last of all, it was covered with a thick mat of clay, well dampened and spread out so as to enclose everything. For the pit had to remain thus, from four to six hours, in other words till evening.

This particular feast was slow in developing, for the men had hardly finished their work when it began to rain. And as the afternoon wore on, the downpour increased to a deluge. The cold slashing rain gradually penetrated the earth around the pit, chilling it much too rapidly for the success of the cooking program, and sank straight through the clay pack.

Opening the pit experimentally toward evening,

the natives found the meat still insufficiently cooked. But, apparently, where there is a will there is a way. And it is remarkable what a good temper most of the natives have. This trouble brought on none of the senseless anger and somewhat unreasoning profanity with which the Anglo-Saxon so often meets such a situation. With sweat and rain running down their faces, they went cheerfully to work, again. They hastily built a shack over the pit to stop the greater part of the rain that was still pouring down, and opening their oven, rearranged the wood and the food and resumed their cooking. As a consequence of this delay the food lay in the ground all night, and the agonized expectations of the hungry lepers danced attendance upon the job. But the obstinacy and skill of the workers gradually got the better of nature, the storm slowly slackened off, and the feast came through with a thoroughness to exceed all expectations.

At four o'clock in the morning the excited fellows rapped at the Sisters' front door, and Mother Marianne and her helpers got ready. From every little cottage, in the wind and dark, emerged the lepers with lanterns and lamps, and an eager party gathered around the *imu*. That time, all came out well. The food was removed carefully, wrapped, and placed in a storeroom to be kept hot. And when the lepers had attended an early Mass and received Communion, the feast was spread.

The Sisters used nine sacks of flour in baking bread, cakes, and cookies, to contribute to the celebration, and Mother Marianne sent one hundred and sixty cakes baked in pint bowls to the boys' Home, besides a huge supply of cookies. She was the better able to accomplish this as the Board of Health had recently sent out a new cookstove.

Unhappily it was such a big stove and so heavy that when it was being heaved over the steamer's side, and landed on the wharf, it tipped, and nearly fell out of the cradle and into the Pacific. Remembering that here the bottom shelves away very quickly and within a few yards of shore is often several hundred feet deep, one can readily imagine that if the new stove had gone to Davy Jones' locker it would have stayed there. The whole available population of the hospital and settlement had watched the debarkation of that stove, and their hearts were in their mouths while they viewed the near mishap. But at last it was hauled safely over the hillside, and brought in, and then the men had to tear out one side of the cook-house, for no door would admit the huge piece. Much excitement had prevailed amongst the lepers, the cats scurried about the yard spitting and screeching, with their tails over their backs, and the little gamin children howled and cheered, and the new stove got in safely.

The big baking at Easter was its baptism into service, so to speak. Shellfish, *poi*, fried cakes, biscuits, and coffee, were added to the other rations. Mother Marianne decorated the dining room, and ushered the patients in.

It rained torrents during the forenoon, and the sky grew black. Water ran in sudden brooks across the lawns, and every gully poured its roaring foaming rivulet into the sea, but as for the lepers sitting warm and dry beside little fires and eating away with a calculated indiscretion, since Easter comes but once a year, nothing could dampen their spirits. It was a good Easter after all.

XIII

THE LAST DAYS AND DEATH
OF MOTHER MARIANNE

ALTHOUGH Mother Marianne had been sick for years, and had suffered a great deal, she lived almost to the age of eighty-three, and from the time she made her profession until shortly before her death, she had always certain responsible charges in the community. In spite of a severe cough, and repeated hemorrhages, she remained determinedly at her post.

In a letter on May 9, 1911, to Reverend Mother M. Johanna, Provincial Superior, she wrote:

"My poor old heart is hungry to have a talk with you, but it is ever the same old story—no time to do so. Please do let me hear from you. . . . In your many hardships and heavy trials you have my deepest and most heartfelt sympathy. Many times daily my thoughts are with you, and then a fervent prayer goes to God that He may have you in His holy keeping and bless you with strength and light for your arduous duties.

"I am doing well for me, but my courage fails me often when I see so much that should be done, and I find myself

too weak to do it. Thank God the Sisters are good to me.
May God love them for all their sweet charity to me. . . .
    "All send *Aloha* to you, dear Mother,
                "Your most devoted Sister Marianne."

She afforded, indirectly a good clue to her own
position and the demands it made upon her, when
she said one day to Sister Leopoldina, with reference
to her own failing powers, "I wish Sister Benedicta
to take my place. I have always had her in view
for the work. She is so self-sacrificing and courage-
ous, there is nothing too hard for her. She shrinks
from nothing. I know she will be able to continue
the work."

Perhaps Mother Marianne did not think of it in
just this way, but what she said about the difficulties
of the work and the fearful demands it would make
upon the worker explained with terrible clarity what
she herself had done and was doing. Someone was
needed to continue the task who would, literally,
wear herself out in the effort. There was no hint of
self-pity in the remarks, no indication that anything
out of the ordinary had been accomplished, only that
she and her fellow workers were standing at their
posts. It is an unusual attitude in the world of today
among so many people seeking the *quid pro quo*, and
has an element of the fine as well as the unusual.

She never lost interest in what was going on

around her. And as usual her thoughts were largely for her helpers. In a letter to her General Superior, Reverend Mother M. Margaret, at Syracuse, N. Y., April 28, 1914, she says in part:

"I am poorly, cannot [do] much, but am up and about directing and helping the poor Sisters. All are hard workers, have been for years. Sister Crescentia has been in the Hawaiian Islands since 1883, Sister Leopoldina since 1885, Sister Antonella since 1888, and Sister Elizabeth came to us as a helper in 1884. She came direct from the ship that brought her family from Madeira. All these years she has been our cook. She is worn out and cannot work much longer.

"Please, dear Mother, consider this is a hastily written business letter and kindly excuse it—the mail man is waiting—All send love to you, dear Mother, and to all the dear Sisters—You are all remembered in our daily prayers."

Then her powers began to fail rapidly. On October 3, 1916, she wrote in a brief letter to another Sister:

"I manage to get about four hours sleep every night. Consequently I am poorly."

In *Scribner's Magazine* for July, 1916, Katharine Fullerton Gerould wrote a description of a visit to Kalaupapa, and thus referred to the heroine of Molokai:

Last Days and Death

"Mother Marianne, in her little parlor, was the blood-kin of all superiors I have ever known; the same soft yellowed skin with something both tender and sexless in the features; the same hint of latent authority in the quiet manner; the same gentle aristocratic gayety; the same tacit endeavor to make human pity co-terminous with God's.

"Like other superiors I have known from childhood up, she seemed an old, old woman who had seen many things. It was only when one stopped to think of the precise nature of those things which, in thirty years on Molokai, Mother Marianne has seen, that the breath failed for an instant.

"The parlor was half filled with garments ready to be given out to lepers, and if one but glanced through the window, one saw the pitiful figures on the cottage porches across the compound. Yet those eyes of hers might have been looking out on a Gothic cloister this half century."

It should be remembered that when this account was written Mother Marianne was nearly eighty years of age, and had lost long since the brilliance and beauty that had distinguished her in youth and even far into middle age. Curiously enough, she seemed to like this published account. Friends sent it to her, and she read it with interest, and retained it thereafter.

In September of 1916, Sister Benedicta was summoned from her work with the Kapiolani girls and came to Molokai. Mother Marianne was not obliged to remain in her room, but had become very weak, and quite unequal now to the wearisome tasks that had claimed all her attention in the past. When Sister Benedicta took charge of the Bishop Home, Mother Marianne was released to a considerable extent from her previous routine.

She had worked hard and steadily at her usual tasks up, almost, to the moment when she was superseded. The organism was nearly worn out, but accustomed as it was to the well-worn grooves of habit, it would still swing on to its daily work for a short time. But it seems remarkably true that as a person grows old who has labored very hard, and is now suddenly forced to abandon this labor, the very repose, the rest, the inaction after long strife, destroys more surely than did the previous exertion. Mother Marianne suddenly grew very feeble, and the doctor ordered her taken about in a large rolling chair.

After this, in the intervals of their work, various Sisters and patients volunteered to wheel her about the building, the veranda, and the yard. She went only occasionally amongst the leper children, but her obviously failing powers distressed her patients, who saw in this fact an unwelcome forecast of the inevitable. The natives in particular, to whom death held chiefly the threat of an everlasting injury, an irreparable blow, regarded her gloomily, feeling that in her they would lose a most efficient and unselfish friend.

Last Days and Death

She kept an air of self-possession, with a flash of gay good nature, to the last. One evening she summoned Sister Leopoldina to take her to the veranda once more. It was cool and clear, the air very fresh, and a light breeze rustling in the ironwood trees, and shaking the long boughs. The west was golden and still, like a scene of molten fire grown rigid. She looked at its brilliance a little while.

A leper child ran up, stared into Mother Marianne's face, and grew deathly pale. Tears filled her eyes, she started to speak, choked, and stood still, sobbing. She knew with the terrible intuition of childhood, what was taking place. But Mother Marianne raised her hand, and waved to the little one. The hand fell back helplessly in her lap. "Now, Sister," she said, "to my room."

The Sisters gathered about her, and prayed. She lay very quietly on her bed; no change in facial expression; not a muscle moving; only an almost imperceptible breathing made her chest rise and fall. At a little after eleven o'clock, August 9, 1918, with a faint snapping gesture, an almost unnoticed movement of her shoulders, she passed away. There was silence in the room, broken at intervals by the low crying of some of the patients and younger Sisters.

Mother Marianne was lying still, at the end of her long journey.

The funeral was held at four o'clock on the following afternoon. The lepers of Molokai united all classes, races, and creeds in the procession that was their last direct opportunity to do her honor. Following the services, the lepers knelt around her grave and prayed for her.

The grave, originally, was intended to be very close to the Damien monument, but because of the rocky character of the soil, this plan had to be abandoned, and the site was moved a little farther away. A grave there would have necessitated the blasting away of so much stone that a great expenditure of time and effort would have been entailed, with also a likelihood of damaging the monument. At the foot of a little side hill, on which is an orange grove and other trees which Mother Marianne herself had planted, and tenderly cared for with her own hands the grave was dug. The lot is only a few paces from the roadside, and just inside the wall are huge ironwood trees that rustle in the cool ocean breeze. The sun shines warm and clear, and the great clouds, misty and white, hang motionless over the Pacific.

XIV

PRESENT WORK OF THE SISTERS OF SAINT FRANCIS IN THE HAWAIIAN ISLANDS

MOTHER MARIANNE's was the first death among the Sisters who went to Molokai, and true to her prediction neither she nor any of her Sisters ever contracted leprosy. To her staff that still carries on the work, she is not gone, but in spirit is with them and directs them. The greatest single thing, I think, that she accomplished was to make the victims understand that they were not utterly outcasts abandoned by the world, but that some people, many people, really loved them.

The inscription on her monument reads "In memory of Reverend Mother Marianne, born January 23, 1838, died August 9, 1918. R. I. P. Erected by the people of the Settlement."

It is a slender and graceful memorial, and in keeping with its unusual art has that direct simplicity that bespeaks genius. It represents the crucified Christ reaching down from his cross to embrace a Brother, and every line of it is tense with vivid energy and a taut nervous eagerness. It has a message not readily forgotten, and alluding as it does to Mother Marianne's own sacrifice is doubly touching.

Commenting upon her death Brother Dutton writes as follows:

BALDWIN HOME,
Kalawao, Dec. 7, 1918.

SISTER M. BENEDICTA,
Bishop Home,
DEAR SISTER:

An interesting letter came yesterday from Dr. McCoy. I quote here for you a bit of it. "I cannot tell you how I appreciate your sending me the little souvenir in the handwriting of Mother Marianne, one whom I am proud to have known and considered a friend. We are better men and women for having come in contact with such a lovely character as she was. I appreciate also your sending the letter over to the Sisters—in addition to telephoning them."

Aloha, sincerely,
(signed) JOSEPH DUTTON.

In discussing the present (1934) status of the Sisters' work, it is only right to begin with the focal point of all interest, Molokai. The very character of the terrain has undergone strong alterations since Mother Marianne first set foot in Kalaupapa. There was a day when the sun-baked grisly plain shivered in the heat waves, the wind tossed little "dust devils" everywhere along the roads, and not a great tree or shrub broke the monotonous level of the prairie's sterility around Bishop Home. The tall pali still rise behind the settlement, and the sea rumbles and thunders on the abbreviated beach, but there are trees and shrubs, groves and woodlots, where before there was desolation. Flowers and gardens, American and foreign plants, some exotic, some from temperate and hardy zones, flourish in the settlements, beside the houses and by the roads. The original desert-like character of the lonely tongue of land is crushed.

Encouraged by the trees and water, the people have gardened. There is food produced now in plenty, small crops flourish. It is a long step on the difficult road to a spiritual and physical contentment. The red dust roads do not glare in one's eyes as they did; soft green vegetation sprinkles the plain.

Where Damien saw only rocky crags and windy open spaces, there are now well-ordered settlements, cottages for the lepers, and separate homes for the leprous men and women who will accept nursing care from the Sisters. Hospitals stand where there was once no pretense at scientific treatment, and doctors study the reports sent out by investigators on the ground. Though the enemy is not beaten, and indeed with difficulty is held at bay, he is at least retained in check, and bit by bit medical science seems to be narrowing down his hiding places and closing in upon him. The use of chaulmoogra oil, long known in its cruder forms, received great impetus but a few years ago from the successful investigations of an American negro girl student, who was working for a degree of Master of Arts in Chemistry in the University of Honolulu, and who perhaps worked out the first decisive steps toward the long awaited cure; certainly the medicine devised if not a positive cure has given the disease strong opposition. The outlook from the medical point of view is not so rosy as optimistic newspapermen would have us believe, but it is at least improved over that of former years, and there are indications that the day may be near at hand on which this destructive plague may itself be destroyed. On December 31, 1890, there were 1,213 lepers in the custody of the Board of Health, the highest number ever reached. Today, roughly, the account is cut in half.

The whole situation is more hopeful, and unstinted credit is due to the Sisters of Saint Francis whose work amongst the victims has made much of this medical research possible. Today there is in the leper settlement the best spirit that has ever prevailed. True, owing to the poverty of the government, and owing too to difficulties over which the devoted nurses have no control, the work in the leper colony still falls short of that near-perfection usually demanded, and often practically attained, in great American hospitals. But medical and surgical facilities are greatly advanced; most of all, there is the human element; loving assistance, intelligent sympathy. This, in large measure, the Sisters have supplied.

About a year after Mother Marianne's death, one notes that in the report of the president of the Board of Health for the year ending June 30, 1919, that leprosy is rated twelfth among the fifteen chief causes of death in the Territory; as it occasioned 60 deaths that year, or a rate of .23 per one thousand population. Beriberi preceded and syphilis followed leprosy in the list. Tuberculosis, leprosy, and measles were on the increase, though the leprous gain was negligible. Of leprosy Oahu reported 45 cases, Maui 39, Hawaii 20, Kauai 6, a total of 110.

The number of cases at the leper settlement, Kalawao, was 611, an increase of 3 over the previous year. The nationalities of the lepers varied widely; American, Belgian, Chinese, Japanese, Philippino, Porto Rican, Spanish, German, Korean cases stand side by side. Even the far New Hebrides Islands contribute their share.

Three 80-gallon hot water tanks were installed that year, and in the Bishop Home two bath tubs.

There is a certain grim humor in these dry government reports, not placed there by the compilers assuredly, but inherent in the incongruities so indifferently listed. Thirteen Kalawao couples ventured into the holy bonds of matrimony during that twelve months, and fifteen children were born in the settlement, most of them of leprous parents. It also appeared that there were 60 horses and 25 donkeys whose ownership could not be determined, as they were in each case claimed by two or more individuals, and the title still in dispute.

In passing, there is a paragraph worth noting: "The Committee regret the apparent uselessness of the Federal Leprosarium at Kalawao, which, after the expenditure of large sums of money, is not used by anyone, and seems to be gradually going to decay, to which its exposed position on a high bluff on the seashore directly in the path of the trade winds and sea spray, is only a further help (page 54)."

Sir Arthur Quiller-Couch once wrote a pleasant little story called "Two Sides of the Face." One is reminded forcibly of that significant title every time he looks at the records of leprosy in our territories, for side by side with the most unselfish devotion and the noblest sacrifice go some of the most perfect specimens of greed, selfishness, ignorance, and cheating. Clearly the millennium is still eluding us.

The Sisters of Saint Francis

In the report of 1929 it is recorded that the old Federal Leprosarium has been torn down, and the materials used in part to repair buildings at Kalaupapa, so the money originally squandered there has finally, in part, gone to a good purpose.

The water supply is still the subject of comment. The long pipe line, much of it passing along the seafront, and exposed to wind and storm, has repeatedly broken, and thus subjected patients depending upon it to great hardship.

But in a material and constructive way, the Sisters' work has flourished. Honolulu is proud of the St. Francis training school for girls, also called the Novitiate of the Sisters of Saint Francis. Here, young women receive training that enables them to devote their lives to God, and to their neighbors for His sake, to nurse the sick, and to teach and care for the children, and similar duties. At Hilo is the St. Joseph School for Girls, an elementary and Junior High School, with a convent and chapel adjacent; grades being in the usual branches.

At Wailuku on Maui is the Maui children's home, built by the people of Maui, and but recently given up, and St. Anthony's school for girls. Then, the Bishop Home at Kalaupapa, where since 1888 the Sisters have cared, and are now caring, for leprous women and girls. And, too, the Kapiolani Home, now located on a beautiful site on the slope of a mountain, overlooking the sea and some of the suburbs of Honolulu. And St. Francis Hospital, the only Catholic hospital in the Vicariate.

But the clearest note of appreciation for Mother Marianne and for the Franciscan Sisters, is struck by the leprous people of Kalaupapa, Molokai. The most touching tribute to the labors of the Sisters is the lepers' donation of over twelve hundred dollars toward the new convent in Honolulu, a contribution not perhaps large as compared with those in our great and wealthy cities, but wonderful from the standpoint of the poor, the infirm, and the sick.

This money was accompanied by a letter to Mother Bernadette, who is now in charge of Saint Francis Novitiate, Honolulu. This letter deserves quotation in full.

Kalaupapa, Molokai, July 18, 1929.

THE REVEREND MOTHER M. BERNADETTE,
Saint Francis Novitiate,
Honolulu, T. H.

DEAR MOTHER BERNADETTE:

As a token of appreciation of the self sacrificing work carried on by the Sisters of Saint Francis in the Kalaupapa settlement for the past forty-one years, and the care and mothering of our children over a period of forty-four years, we take sincere pleasure in forwarding the enclosed

The Sisters of Saint Francis

$1,284.43 representing donations, collections, and earnings from charity Fair and Concert of July 13, as our donation to a fund for the purpose of building a home in Honolulu for the Sisters of Saint Francis.

It is our earnest hope and prayer that our donation will prove to be the cornerstone upon which will be built a fund large enough to insure the early completion of a Home which will stand as a monument commemorating the work of our beloved Mother Marianne and the Sisters of Saint Francis.

Aloha nui loa,

The People of Kalaupapa by their committee.
(Signed) ALOYSIUS KAMAKA (Catholic), *Chairman.*
(Mrs.) MARY HALEARNAN (Mormon).
(Mrs.) NANCY HORE (Catholic).
JACK KAMEALOHA (Calvinist).

The simple story of Barbara Kopp is soon told, but the influences that this remarkable woman set in motion, and the results accomplished are still growing and spreading in the country where she died. Her life and her triumph on Molokai are another link in the long chain of proofs which human experience forges, that soul does triumph over body, and the materialist and sceptic yield to the charitable effort of honest toil. It is easy to be sceptical and indifferent when one is far away and comfortable; it is another thing to see at first hand what these lonely women confronted and defeated; solitude, crime, disease, despair, starvation, desertion, and misery.

Mother Marianne's monument is a beautiful memorial to a great soul. It is like a quiet strain that closes a long and magnificent symphony; every tone from safest comfort to deepest danger has sounded, and in the end of life there is peace and repose after labor.

Robert Louis Stevenson's little Requiescat occurs readily:

> *Under the wide and starry sky*
> *Dig the grave and let me lie;*
> *Glad have I lived and gladly die*
> *And I lay me down with a will.*

Mother Marianne has her reward. She is a ceaseless inspiration to her companion Sisters to carry on the work, a reminder to folk of other creeds and climes and races that goodness and truth, honesty and sincerity, have still their honored place; that the world is not given over to the devils of selfishness, falsehood, and treachery, however much pessimists may say so, and that mankind still looks to spiritual guidance for all that is best and finest in death or in life.

"She is not dead, but sleepeth."

APPENDIX A

MOTHER MARIANNE'S APPOINTMENTS
IN NEW YORK

On June 11, 1864, the Definitorium elected Mother
Marianne Vicaria of the St. Francis Convent, Syracuse,
N. Y.; and in July, 1865, Vicaria of St. Anthony Convent
of the same city; and on January 15, 1866, she received
appointment as temporary superior of the Convent at
Rome, N. Y., from the Very Reverend Commissary Gen-
eral. On August 3, 1866, the Definitorium elected her
Superior at St. Teresa's Convent, the new mission at
Oswego, N. Y. This appointment she held until August 14,
1868, when the Very Reverend Fidelis Dehm, Commissary
General, appointed her Superior of St. Clare's Convent,
Utica, N. Y. On November 10, 1869, the Definitorium
chose her to return as Superior to St. Teresa's Convent,
Oswego, N. Y. This appointment was to have been for
three years, but in June, 1870, the Very Reverend Com-
missary General transferred her as Superior to St. Joseph's
Hospital, Syracuse, N. Y. On December 28, 1871, Mother
Marianne became Novice Mistress and Secretary of the
Order, but the Very Reverend Fidelis Dehm, Commissary
General, again appointed her Superior of St. Joseph's Hos-
pital. On December 29, 1874, she again received election
as Novice Mistress and Secretary of the Order, which office

she held until April 26, 1875, when at the order of the Provincial Mother she went a third time to St. Joseph's Hospital, Syracuse, N. Y.

This list of appointments will give a fair idea of the executive work thrust upon this woman year after year, of the manner in which she was shifted from one responsibility to another, and of the genuine need felt for her services.

APPENDIX B

A NOTE ON LEPROSY

A NOTE upon leprosy, somewhat more detailed than the running account in the text would warrant, is here appended.

Briefly, there are two fairly distinct types of the disease, which often tend to mingle and form a third type. All of these with their various symptoms may be identified rather readily.

Nodular leprosy is characterized at first by an outbreak of red spots which later become pigmented and thickened. These spots come out in crops, increasingly red with the attacks of irregular fever, soon taking on the appearance of limited areas of sunburn. They vary in size from one or two millimetres to a blotch as large as the palm of the hand. They are raised and usually appear on the lobes of the ears, the lateral projections of the nose, the forehead, the eyebrows, the cheeks, and the chin. The muscular surfaces of the forearms, thighs, and buttocks are also favorite sites. The palms of the hands, soles of the feet, hairy scalp, groin, and axillary regions, are almost never attacked. These spots may be supersensitive at first, but they soon show complete loss of sense of pain and sense of temperature, although retaining the sense of touch. These spots, furthermore, do not sweat, but remain dry even in a general perspiration.

Following successive attacks of fever and reappearances of spots, reddish-brown nodular masses are developed usually on the sites of the spots. These nodules are elastic to the touch, and due to an active fatty secretion have a greasy appearance. These protruding nodules, moreover, may give the face a leonine appearance, whence the name *leontiasis,* or the appearance of a satyr, whence *satyriasis.* With the development of the nodules the hair falls out of the eyebrows and bearded face. When they develop in the mucous membranes of the nose, mouth, and larynx, they cause offensive discharges, difficulty in breathing and eating, and a raucous voice.

The eye is involved with frightful frequency in this form of leprosy. The eyelids, conjunctivæ, cornea and iris are unfiltrated with subsequent ulceration and loss of sight. The nodules on the face, back of hands, buttocks, etc., may disappear by resolution, but the tendency is for them to ulcerate and produce contractures and deformities. The glands in the region of the lesions become enlarged but do not tend to form matter. Visceral involvements are not common, but serious lesions of the liver have been reported. A much disputed question is that of leprotic involvement of the lungs. This is probably rare, but seems to have occurred.

The course of the disease is essentially chronic, and unless some intercurrent affliction carries off the patient, the end comes with a general physical collapse after some years.

It is very difficult, almost impossible to set accurate figures to the length of time required for the disease to run its course. There is such a wide variation in human beings, in their constitutions, in their powers of resistance, and in their susceptibilities to various attacks, that an average is hard to draw. A leprous condition that would kill one man within two years may not bring death to another for ten years. This is one of the truly horrible facets of this hard and impenetrable problem; the time required for dying is some times lengthened to an almost incredible degree. Father Damien may have had the disease nearly thirteen years before he died; other men who seemed even larger, stronger, and more enduring than the priest, succumbed within a few months.

Toward the latter stages, the patient's temperature gradually falls, and a state of coma usually ushers in the end. But when nerve leprosy sets in upon the nodular type, the life of the patient seems to be prolonged.

The symptomatic manifestations of nerve leprosy are caused by the irritation of the nerve fibres, by infected tissue, and are chiefly neuralgic pains and sensory disturbances such as itching and loss of feeling in the external organs of sense. The ulnar, perneal, and facial nerves are particularly attacked, but the process very rarely extends above the knee or elbow. An anæsthesia of the region controlled by the ulnar nerve, with contractions of the fourth and fifth fingers, may be symptoms of nerve leprosy. In those cases where the appearance of smooth yellowish-brown spots precede the neuritic manifestations, anæsthesia may also be present, provided the eruption has lasted for some time.

The fully developed case of nerve leprosy shows anæsthetic spots, tropic lesions of the skin and bone, together with muscular palsies. The spots often appear singly and may be from one-half to several inches in diameter. They are not raised, but have a sunburnt color, and do not sweat. Instead of having a preference for the exposed parts, they appear most frequently on the covered portions of the body, such as trunk, buttocks, scapular region, thighs, and arms, although the first appearance of spots may be on the face. These spots often look like ringworm lesions, having a very red border with a paler center, but they are oval in outline, rather than round, and there is no scaling. Blisterous eruptions, which are most frequently noted about the knuckles and are often followed by ulcerations, are rare manifestations of nerve leprosy.

As the disease progresses, the nerve trunks begin to enlarge, especially the ulnar at the elbow, and the great auricular as it crosses the sternomastoid muscle. The characteristic nerve enlargement is spindle-shaped or beaded. These nerve enlargements are at first tender but later become painless, and the patient exhibits extensive areas of anæsthesia and tropic changes of the skin and nails of fingers and toes, such as felons, glazed skin, brillæ, the last of which eventually rupture and leave ulcers. The phalangeal bones may be completely absorbed and a distorted nail cap the end of a metacarpal bone. Owing to the anæsthesia, lepers often burn or otherwise injure their fingers and toes. Perforating ulcers are more common in leprosy than general decay.

Muscular palsies, atrophies and contractures are more common in the face and upper extremity than in the lower extremity. Of the facial muscles the orbicularis palpabrarum is most likely to show paralysis. The eyes are affected much less frequently in nerve leprosy than in nodular, about forty-five percent as opposed to about eighty-five percent in nodular types. The most common changes in nerve leprosy are the turning outward of the lower lid and subsequent ulceration of the outer surface.

A Note on Leprosy

In mixed leprosy there is simply a combination of the manifestations of the two main types. As a matter of fact, the majority of cases tend eventually to assume a mixed type.

APPENDIX C

MR. GIBSON AND THE CHARTER
OF INCORPORATION

REGARDING the incorporation and definite establishment of the Franciscan Sisters in Hawaii, the following letter written by Walter M. Gibson to Fr. Joseph Lesen, the then Provincial Minister of the Franciscan Fathers, who was guiding the Sisters' community, will be of interest.

Department of Foreign Affairs,
Honolulu, H. I., Feb. 12, 1887.

DEAR and REV'D FATHER:

I duly received your valued letter of Aug. 23, 1886, and I delayed further correspondence until there had been confirmation of a certain matter in behalf of the Franciscan Sisters established in this Kingdom. Of this I am happy to give you assurance by enclosing a certified copy of a charter to incorporate the Third Franciscan Order in this Kingdom. It is now my purpose, and I shall have the assistance of His Majesty King Kalakaua and the Hawaiian Government, to establish the Sisters under the guidance of Mother Marianne in a Home or Mother House in Honolulu, which will be their own property as a chartered religious community. The King and Queen and all classes rejoice in the establishment of these ladies in the country as a blessing to the Hawaiian people. I am proud to have had a part in bringing them here, and I shall deem it one of the most important of the duties of my life, and the most exalted of its pleasures, to continue to assist in the establishment and comfortable settlement of the Franciscan Sisterhood in this Kingdom.

Be pleased to accept, dear and Reverend Father, the assurances of the profound regard and respect, of,

(Signed) WALTER M. GIBSON.

APPENDIX D

MOTHER MARIANNE'S BIRTH DATE

THERE still exist some uncertainties regarding the early life of this remarkable woman. Her birth date is given commonly from the archives of St. Anthony's Convent, Syracuse, N. Y., as January 23, 1838, but that figure is disputed, and for various reasons 1836 is suggested as the year, instead of 1838.

I have chosen 1836 for two reasons.

It is agreed by all accounts that Barbara Kopp was about a year and a half old when the family emigrated from Germany. Now, all the original members of the family are dead, and for that matter most of the sons and daughters of the original members are also dead.

There is one surviving nephew to Mother Marianne, Mr. Lerscholl, 2000 Lodi Street, Syracuse, N. Y., a man now sixty-four years of age, a brother to Father Alphonse Lerscholl. Mr. Lerscholl is the son of Mother Marianne's sister, Eva. It was to Father Alphonse Lerscholl, who died in Trenton, N. J., in 1929, that Sr. Magdalene, the sister nurse who attended Mother Marianne during her last illness, wrote the account concerning the death.

The letter is dated at one o'clock in the morning, August 10, 1918, at Kalaupapa, Molokai, and reads in part: "Before these few lines reach you, you will most likely have heard of the death of our dearly beloved Mother Marianne, as the Sisters intend to cable to Syracuse in the morning. . . . She died a holy death at 11 P.M., August 9th. . . . She had been very ill for a long time and bore her ailments very patiently as was her nature. . . . Last week, Friday, she asked Sr. M. Benedicta to have me come to help care for her, for she knew how anxious I was to see her. But there was no steamer due until Thursday morning, so they wirelessed to Honolulu to have the *Claudine* stop for Sr. M. Benedicta at Kaunakakai, and she walked up that awful pali (referring to the 2,500 foot cliff that cuts off access to the leper settlement, and which is crossed only by a single footpath, frequently rendered impassable by storms and always precarious even in daylight) and boarded a sampan which took her out to mid-ocean to the *Claudine* and came to Wailuku for me. And we returned the same way, and came down the pali by moonlight. . . . One such experience is quite enough for a lifetime, but I believe I would do it again if I could be of any service to Mother. . . . She was taken to her last resting place, which is about 150 feet from Father Damien's monument, which is on the Bishop Home grounds as you will probably remember. They tried to dig a grave right next to the monument, but it was almost solid rock, so they made it as near as they could find the earth soft enough to do it."

Now, this Mr. Lerscholl, basing his accounts on his recollection of what his mother, Eva Kopp Lerscholl, told him, is certain that the emigration to Utica occurred in 1837. If that date is correct, 1836 is almost certainly the year of birth. There is also in the archives of the Franciscan Sisters an old account of the chief events of Mother Marianne's life, an account gathered by an unnamed Sister, which apparently does not indicate sources but also gives 1836 as the birth date.

No consolation can be gathered from baptismal records, for strangely enough there is no record of Mother Marianne's baptism filed in the archives of the St. Anthony Convent.

Mr. Lerscholl is certain that the original family name was Kopp. This tallies with Mother Marianne's own spelling, but it is incorrectly given in many sources as Kob. Perhaps because there are similarities in the sounds of B and P, in German, when rapidly pronounced, and the new neighbors of the immigrant family in Utica may not have learned the name accurately. Some of the descendants are now spelling it Cope.

The fact that the baptismal record is missing is very extraordinary, as usually no one is received into the Order without it. There is a record, however, that she received her First Communion in St. John's Church, Utica, N. Y., so that clearly her pastor felt satisfied of the genuineness of her religious standing. As every indication points to the devotion of her parents, one may safely assume that the archive note on baptism is correct, even though the certificate itself is not at hand.

APPENDIX E

FRANCISCAN SISTERS NOW ON DUTY IN HAWAII

St. Francis Convent (the Mother Marianne Memorial)
2707 Pamoa Road, Honolulu, T. H.

Mother M. Bernadette
Sr. M. Leopoldina Burns
Sr. M. Cyrilla
Sr. M. Louis

Sr. M. Elizabeth Gomez *
Sr. M. Julia
Sr. M. Thecla
Sr. M. Gonzaga

St. Francis Hospital, Liliha Street, Honolulu, T. H.

Sr. M. Eugenia, Sup.
Sr. M. Antonia
Sr. M. Lidwina
Sr. M. Jolenta
Sr. M. Herman Joseph

Sr. Joseph Mary
Sr. M. Pancratia
Sr. M. Teresa
Sr. M. Joseph
Sr. M. Ignatia (patient)

Kapiolani Girls' Home, 1650 Meyer Street
Honolulu, T. H.

Sr. M. Benedicta, Sup.
Sr. M. Albina
Sr. M. Eymard
Sr. Miriam

Sr. Marie Celine
Sr. M. Imelda
Sr. M. Anna

* The Sister Elizabeth Gomez, now on duty at St. Francis Convent, is the same Sister Elizabeth who was a little girl called Olinda Gomez, when Mother Marianne went to Molokai.

Mother Marianne of Molokai

BISHOP HOME, Kalaupapa, Molokai

Mother M. Flaviana, Sup.   Sr. M. Martha
Sr. M. Praxedes   Sr. M. Marianne

SACRED HEART CONVENT, Lahaina, Maui, T. H.

Sr. M. Beata, Sup.   Sr. M. Colette
Sr. M. Philomena   Sr. M. Antoinette

ST. JOSEPH CONVENT, Hilo, Hawaii, T. H.

Sr. M. Teresa, Sup.   Sr. M. Martina
Sr. M. Adelaide   Sr. M. Flora
Sr. Leonilda   Sr. M. Irene
Sr. Isabella   Sr. M. Liberta
Sr. Margaret Mary   Sr. M. Francis

These names represent forty-three Sisters assigned to the respective mission in September, 1934; and all present missions.

APPENDIX F

BISHOP HOME'S RULES

HEREWITH are appended some of the rules established by Superintendent T. E. Evans for the Leper Settlement. They may be of interest, as showing how the Bishop Home was conducted.

1. No inmate of the Home shall leave the premises without permission from the proper authorities.

2. All labor necessary to the conducting of the Establishment shall be performed by the inmates, without compensation other than their food and clothing.

3. The whole number of able-bodied inmates of the Home shall be divided into four distinct gangs or bodies. Each of which bodies shall perform the work required of them for one week, and rest three weeks.

4. Cleanliness is expected above all things, and each room must be thoroughly cleansed by the inmates thereof every day.

5. Any person found trespassing upon the grounds of the Home without permission shall be punished.

6. Every inmate of the Home must be on the premises not later than 6 o'clock P.M., unless he has special permission to absent himself after that hour.

7. The strictest obedience to those in authority is ex-

pected, and will be exacted of the inmates. Any disobedience will be punished.

8. Whenever any inmate of the Home shall deem himself aggrieved in any way, or shall have cause of complaint against any other inmate or any person whatsoever, he shall immediately go to the Sisters in charge of the Home and lay his grievance or complaint before her, and whatever action she may take in the matter shall be final and decisive.

(Signed) T. E. Evans, *Superintendent.*
Leper Settlement.

Mr. Evans was a political appointee, but he seems to have known his duties thoroughly and executed them with firmness.

APPENDIX G

BIBLIOGRAPHY

CAUDWELL. Damien of Molokai.
  Written somewhat after the fashion of an apologia,
  and rather subjective, but an excellent book.
CURTAYNE. St. Anthony of Padua.
  Brief biographical sketch. Informative as showing the
  Franciscan ideal.
DUTTON. The Samaritans of Molokai.
  Biographical studies of Father Damien and Brother
  Dutton, particularly the latter. Scholarly and well
  written.
MOURITZ. The Path of the Destroyer.
  Leprosy from the standpoint of medical research.
  Excellent.
Reports of the President of the Board of Health of the T.H.
  These reports are printed somewhat irregularly. At
  one time they were brought out every six months.
  They are very detailed, and full of miscellaneous in-
  formation, much of which throws light, indirectly,
  upon leper problems.
STEVENSON. The South Seas.
  This is one of the older books about life in this strange
  part of the world, but there are none better written
  and few in which there is so much keen observation.

7. United States Government Health Reports.
   There is a long list of these documents available, thorough and informative.
8. YZENDOORN. History of the Catholic Missions in the Hawaiian Islands.
   Compiled on the ground from first-hand sources. Written primarily as a source book for students of history. Dependable.

There are many other good books that could be cited. A bibliography about leprosy alone would fill whole books. There are endless works about the South Seas, many well written. However, they do not all add to our knowledge, many merely repeat with subjective variations what many people already know.

The books above cited are mentioned simply because in a particular way they bear upon the matter treated in this book. As for leprosy, if one will read Mouritz, the U. S. Reports on the study of leprosy in Hawaii and other U. S. possessions, and some of the reports of the leprosy congresses held from time to time in various medical centers of the world, he will have all the necessary information.

For social and geographical observation of the South Sea life, and Hawaiian life, Stevenson is as good as any single observer.

INDEX

Index

[200]

Index

Index

Moltke, 49
Mongolian, 39
Mormons, 115
Moselle, 2
Murphy, Sr. M. Antonella, 30,
40, 41, 71, 166

Napoleon, 89
Nash, Sr. M. Renata, 30, 40,
41, 132
Neisser, 17
New Caledonia, 16
New Hebrides, 175
New Zealand, 9
Niihau, 8
Norway, 17
Nuhou, 26
Numbers, 15

Oahu, 8, 175
Oder, 1
Odin, 2
Oliver, Dr., 145, 152
Pacific, 8, 10, 38, 53, 77, 80,
89, 113, 120, 162, 170
Pali, 64
Paris, 9
Phœnician disease, 16
Picpus Fathers, 9
Polynesian, 9, 35
Pompey, 16
Porto Rican, 175
Portuguese, 9, 16, 128

Quiller-Couch, Sir Arthur, 176

Rhine, 1, 2

Rig Veda, 15
Roman, 1, 2
Rossetti, 136

Saint Anthony's Convent, 5, 29
Saint Anthony's School, 177
Saint Elizabeth Convent, 82
Saint Francis Convent, 5
Saint Francis Training School,
177
Saint Francis Hospital, 178
Saint Helena, 89
Saint Joseph's Hospital, 6, 7
Saint Joseph's School, 177
Saint Mary's Church, 5
Saint Paul, 106
Samoans, 9
Sandwich Islands, 8
San Francisco, 28, 31, 52
Sawaiori, 9
Saxon, 2
South America, 16
South Pacific, 16, 18
South Seas, 10, 11, 80
Stevenson, Robert Louis, 79,
100, 101, 103, 104, 106, 107,
180
Syracuse, 5, 6, 8, 29, 50, 51, 62,
88, 96, 166

Tam O'Shanter, 130
Thurston, L., 76
Tracadie, 27
Trier, 1
Troy, 11
"Typee," 125

Utica, 3

Index